What
EVE
Didn't
Tell Us

What EVE Didn't Tell Us

Sex, Casseroles, and a Life of Faith

•

Sue Thomen Dolquist, M. Div., M. Th.
and Jane M. Wood, Ph. D.

Judson Press
Valley Forge

What Eve Didn't Tell Us
Sex, Casseroles, and a Life of Faith

Judson Press has made every effort to trace the ownership of all quotes. In the event of a question arising from the use of a quote, we regret any error made and will be pleased to make the necessary correction in future printings and editions of this book.

Unless otherwise noted, all Scripture quotations in this volume are from the New Revised Standard Version of the Bible, copyright © 1989 by the Division of Christian Education of the National Council of the Churches of Christ in the United States of America. Used by permission. All rights reserved.

Library of Congress Cataloging-in-Publication Data

Dolquist, Sue Thomen.
    What Eve didn't tell us : sex, casseroles, and a life of faith / Sue Thomen Dolquist and Jane Wood.
    p. cm.
    ISBN 0-8170-1416-0 (pbk. : alk. paper)
    1. Women--Religious life. I. Wood, Jane, 1967- II. Title.

BV4527 .D655 2002
248.8'43--dc21   2001050408

Printed in the U.S.A.

08 07 06 05 04 03 02

10 9 8 7 6 5 4 3 2 1

To my husband, Dan—encourager, partner, and friend
—*Sue Thomen Dolquist*

In memory of Teri McCollum, Ph. D., 1959–2000
—*Jane M. Wood*

Contents

Preface

THIS BOOK IS BOTH A HUMOROUS AND SERIOUS LOOK INTO two women's lives in the modern world. A pastor and a professor, we are women who have achieved a certain measure of success professionally but find we must continuously balance marriage, work, and children in ways that our mothers and grandmothers could not have imagined. This book is our honest and often flawed attempt to share our lives with others in the hope that it will foster laughter and further realizations about the complexity of women's lives in the twenty-first century.

Acknowledgments

MANY THANKS GO TO THE FACULTY AND STAFF OF BAKER University, Overland Park, Kansas, for their insights and financial contributions to the production of this book.

A special thank-you goes to Carolyn Harp and Jenny Thomson for their office support and to the members of Leawood Presbyterian Church in Leawood, Kansas, for their encouragement and enthusiasm for bringing others closer to Christ and for fostering the growth of their pastor.

A debt of gratitude is owed to Ilona and Christine, whose weekly prayers, spiritual encouragement, and faithfulness have given witness to what it is to be a woman of faith.

We also thank our mothers, MaryAnn Vreeland Wood and Phyllis Riley Thomen, for the way they modeled ordinary lives with extraordinary possibilities.

Introduction

TWENTY YEARS AGO, MOST OF US WOULD HAVE ASSUMED THAT a pastor and a professor would be men. Today, that is not the case. We don the robes and the gowns of our professions and move with confidence to the pulpit and the lectern. However, we often struggle to keep balance between attending our children's Halloween parade and attending to the student or parishioner who needs our attention. This volume, which reflects those everyday struggles, endeavors to foster communication, story, and insight into how to bring faith and "real life" into balance.

The voices that we bring to this book are often fragmented, as are our lives. We teach and preach and come home to hungry children, waiting spouses, and the dog that occasionally likes to be noticed. We speak as flawed figures, but also as women who manage to remain married, to participate actively in raising young children, and to show up (usually on time) for work. We trust that you will read this book with a desire to see yourself more clearly, to hear what other women are experiencing, and to balance what we say with how you see the world. It is our hope that the questions following our chapters will allow you individually or in groups, to explore the parts of your life where you need to incorporate balance or to speak out with greater strength. Please know that others out there have been where you are now and that you can be encouraged by those around you to pursue your own dreams and articulate your own struggles.

We are a pastor and a professor. Our perspectives on faith, family, and careers are surprisingly similar in some ways and quite divergent in others. As you read our stories, you will come to know our individual voices, but until then, you may orient yourself to our perspectives by referring to the quotes that open each story. Prof. Jane Wood always leads off with a literary quote from one of the great writers of our past and present. Pastor Sue Dolquist introduces her stories with a brief selection from Scripture. The truth found in literature, whether "sacred" or "secular," is unwavering in its ability to encourage, exhort, and enlighten our response to the world around us. We hope you will continue to strengthen your own voice as you listen to ours.

Father Knows Best

Wisdom gives strength to the wise
more than ten rulers that are in a city.

—*Ecclesiastes 7:19*

MY DAD HAS GIVEN ME THREE DIFFERENT PIECES OF ADVICE
that I remember and revisit from time to time. The first one was
"Remember that it is good to be tall."

I am about five feet eight inches tall, which was certainly
above average when I was in high school. Wearing a size 9 shoe
was unusual then. (I understand that sizes 8 to 8½ are now considered "average.") While I didn't really think about being tall,
my dad continued to tell me what a great thing it was. He
would state the obvious, like "Well, for one, you can see over
other people in a crowd."

My height did come in handy when playing basketball, as I
was able to jump a bit higher since I was already an inch or so
taller than the other players. I must have gone for the taller boys
because I don't recall thinking I had to slouch so I didn't intim-
idate them. Maybe the shorter boys didn't go for me because I
was too tall; I don't remember.

I just have no recollection of my height being an issue. At the
time I wondered why Dad kept telling me that being tall was
good. I just was the height I was, and according to my dad, that

was a good thing. Only now, as I am raising my own daughter, do I see how the words from a father can have such importance. The self-esteem issues of a young woman are complex. The kind words that come from a man she cares about have much to do with how she perceives her own beauty and character. Her father is the first man from whom she seeks approval and recognition. His words can have an enormous impact.

Perhaps the reason I didn't see tallness as an issue is because of the affirmation from my father in previous conversations I don't even remember. I do recall the discussion I had with him when I had started my period for the first time. He and I were on our way out to the country to ride horses. He was driving the formerly green but now canary yellow pickup, and we had both our horses in the canary yellow trailer we were pulling behind us. We were about a mile south of town when he said to me, "Your mother tells me you started your period." I was a bit surprised that he said anything, but not the least bit embarrassed. "Yeah," I replied, as if we were talking about the fact that we needed to buy more oats for the horses. "Well, that means you're growing up," he said. I answered with another "yeah" or nod or equally teenage response. While I must have been embarrassed enough at the time to remember the conversation pretty clearly, I wasn't embarrassed enough to feel like I wanted to roll over and die. I just thought, "Yeah, I'm growing up."

Dad was able to acknowledge my growing into womanhood, affirm me, and make it as comfortable as possible for me. Pretty tricky, I'd say. I wonder how it will be for my daughter when she passes this very strange milestone in a girl's life.

The second piece of advice I can remember my dad telling

me is "You can do anything you want to in life, if you want it badly enough."

Like some folks, I have gone through those years wondering first, "What do I want to be when I grow up?" followed by "What should I pick for a major?" and "What area of specialty should I choose?" and then "What kind of job do I want to work toward?" Despite this wondering, I believed my dad. I am not sure if I was naïve or just supremely confident, but I knew that I could do whatever I wanted to. The caveat that he added, "if you want it badly enough," was key because it meant that I had to work toward my goals, lofty as they might be. I considered the possibility of doctor, lawyer, Indian chief. None of these appealed to me, and I chose a degree in engineering. I chose it because I got good grades in math and science. I chose it because it seemed interesting and challenging. But mostly I chose it because engineers were getting the best job offers at the time I was in college and I wanted to make a lot of money.

I guess making a lot of money was a dream I gave up because I changed my vocation from engineer to pastor. I was called to seminary and didn't look back. Again I chose a male-dominated field and didn't hesitate because I was female or too tall, fat, or ugly. I just did it because I knew I could if I wanted to.

The third piece of advice I received from my father was when I asked him, "So, any words of wisdom before I get married?" He hesitated, thought a bit, and finally said, "Yes. Never try to get even."

I thought about that a bit, and he went on, "Your husband will certainly do something in your marriage that will hurt you, annoy you, depress you, or disappoint you. You can choose how to respond to his mistakes in a lot of different ways. You might get mad, you might pout, you might forgive him, or you might ignore him. But don't try to get even. Don't hurt him because he hurt you. Don't try to even the score. That will only make things worse and probably escalate the problem. You don't have to respond to your pain with more pain."

That was it. "Don't try to get even." This advice has helped me out a few times when we have had "marital moments." If you start down that path, it eventually leads to more hurt for everyone. All this is not to say that I have heeded Dad's advice each time I should have, but I know it to be solid.

I remember one time in particular when the advice could have come in handy had I been grown-up enough to pay attention to it. It is petty, but it makes me chuckle. My husband, Dan, had used the vehicle I normally drive to take a day trip for work. When he returned, he came in the door and said, "You'll need to fill up the van tomorrow; there's no gas in it." He was tired, wanted to get home, and didn't want to stop to get gas— which is very unusual for him. He typically will fill up and sometimes even clean out my van when he uses it.

So the next time I used his car, I did the same thing. Only I did it maliciously, to spite him for doing it to me. And I didn't even tell him until we were both on our way out the door, racing to get to work: "Oh, by the way, your car is running on fumes. I didn't have time to stop yesterday and get gas." So there.

He gave me a blank look and replied softly, "Oh, well, don't you remember that I was taking your van to the shop today to get the brakes worked on, so you were going to drive my car?" Drats. What was that my dad used to say?

The advice I have received from my father has gone a long way to giving me confidence, vision, and a great marriage. Sometimes I even get over myself enough to heed it.

• • •

Feeding Luke to the Wolves (or Not)

And all shall be well and
All manner of thing shall be well....
—*T. S. Eliot, "Little Gidding"*

IN THE RELATIVELY SMALL TOWN WHERE I GREW UP, MY FATHER owned and operated his own accounting business. The difficulties of owning a small business were as much a part of the dinner table as the rolls. By age eleven, while my mother and father discussed the day's happenings, I was busy writing stories in my head. I didn't pay much attention to the "office" stuff.

I was setting the table for my mother one cold evening in February when my dad came home. I saw his face as he walked in, and it looked old and tired. He put his briefcase down next to the door and said to my mother, "Had a bad one today."

My mother put the food on the table, and he sat down heavily, unseeing.

"What happened?" I asked.

My father looked only at my mother as the story unfolded. It seemed that one of his accounts was a small manufacturing plant. Three brothers had inherited the business from their father, and it had served the family well. The two older brothers,

5

"Matthew" and "Mark," had managed the office administration and sales. The youngest brother, "Luke," supervised the blue-collar workers who made the product. For a number of reasons, the business had been losing money for the last few years. The older brothers, who knew more about the business angle, decided to offer the entire business to the younger brother for a "fair" price. They had contacted their lawyer, who had drawn up the contracts. Luke had come into my father's office that day and told him, "Don, I trust you. Will you look these over and tell me what you think?" My father had said that he would.

Dad looked at my mother over the dinner table. "They're selling him down the river," he told my mother. "The numbers have been misrepresented. It's not illegal, but it's unethical."

"So just tell him," I ordered my father with all the authority of an eleven-year-old.

He glanced my way, shook his head. "If I tell him the truth, then I will lose Matthew and Mark's business. Their attorney, 'Paul,' sends me referrals. In a business like mine," he told me, "your reputation is about all you've got."

Dad turned back to my mother and said, "If he buys the business, I could help him get it turned around, spend some time down there with him. It might mean that I'd be gone even more."

My mother, ever practical, asked, "Do you think it can make money again?"

My dad sighed, "I don't know." And then, "No." He pushed his plate away and finished his iced tea. "It's too far in debt." His eyes roamed over the table, paused briefly at my face, and then noted the empty chairs. My four older brothers and sisters were all in college; my oldest brother was due to graduate in the spring.

"If I tell him," he muttered, "we could lose everything."

All of a sudden I felt funny. My bravado was gone, and my stomach felt empty, aching. I liked my house, my family, our life, the way it was. My father, tall and proud, looked almost broken. Our lives seemed as precarious, as easily lost, as the leaves that still occasionally blew up against my bedroom window during a storm.

My mother said quietly, "What are you going to do?"

"I don't know," he said. He left the table and went to the bedroom, closing the door.

"Don't you have homework?" my mother asked.

I nodded and went to my bedroom.

I don't think my father slept much that night.

The next day I was watching reruns of *M*A*S*H* when I heard the garage door open. I walked noiselessly toward the kitchen as Dad came in. I heard my mother say, "Well?"

He leaned his back against the kitchen door. "I couldn't do it," he said angrily. "Dammit, MaryAnn, I couldn't feed Luke to the wolves."

From somewhere inside me I felt a sense of relief, but part of my knot of worry remained. I asked, "Will you lose the business, Dad?"

He shrugged. "I don't know. We called them from my office, and they weren't happy. If I start to lose more clients, then I'll have to go back to work for someone else."

I was horrified. My father had worked every Saturday and nights until seven or eight to "get the business off the ground."

He said to me as he sat down, "If I can't stay in the business with my integrity, then I'll just have to lose it."

He buttered his roll. We ate dinner.

My father retired many years ago. He lost some clients after that night, but he gained some too. When I was in high school, a friend of mine said that he had heard his father say that my dad had a reputation as an "honest" man. My father kept his business until he retired and then passed it on to my brother. But those two nights have stayed with me.

My father was not and is not a perfect man. I am not, nor will ever be, in any way perfect, but whenever I have found myself faced with a moral dilemma, I have said to myself, "I come from a family where we don't feed Luke to the wolves." And it has meant, for the most part, standing up for people, for what I believe in, often in the face of societal disapproval.

I have told my children the story of those two nights so many times that they are beginning to roll their eyes. But I want them to know. I want them to know that in the lonely, dark winter when I was eleven my father gave me one of the greatest gifts a parent can give a child. He risked his income, his business, and his family's future to do right by another human being.

That night, as my father agonized over the decision, he set not only his own path, but he set the rudder for my life as well. And while it has not always been clear sailing, I have mostly been able to keep my face to the forefront with strength and pride. We are not, you see, the kind of people who feed Luke to the wolves.

Following in the Footsteps: Points to Ponder

1. Describe a crisis in your family. How did your parents/guardians respond? How did this response affect you?

2. What good advice have you received in your life? Did you heed it? Explain.

3. What bad examples have you witnessed or bad advice have you received? If you were to counsel someone today, what would you tell a fourteen-year-old girl? a sixty-five-year-old woman? yourself?

4. Do you believe in something so strongly that you would be willing to risk your livelihood for it? What is it?

5. Ecclesiastes 9:17-18 says,

   The quiet words of the wise are more to be heeded
   than the shouting of a ruler among fools.
   Wisdom is better than weapons of war,
   but one bungler destroys much good.

   Have you experienced the truth of these verses in your life? How?

6. Joshua 24:15 reads, "Now if you are unwilling to serve the LORD, choose this day whom you will serve, whether the gods your ancestors served in the region beyond the River or the gods of the Amorites in whose land you are living; but as for me and my household, we will serve the LORD." How would you apply this verse to your family?

Caving in to Grease

It might be true that I remember a time when feminism meant that a woman, although she liked and lusted after men, wanted to be in charge of her own life and her own job and her own carburetor.
—*Cynthia Heimel,* If You Can't Live without Me, Then Why Aren't You Dead Yet?

LAST SATURDAY NIGHT A FRIEND AND I TOOK OUR DAUGHTERS to see *Grease* at the outdoor community theater. It was packed. There were people sitting on lawn chairs, blankets, and sidewalks. There were young people, old people, and all sorts of in-between people. We spread our blankets on an appropriate part of the hill and commenced to eat a picnic supper. The kids chattered happily amidst deviled eggs and peanut butter and jelly sandwiches and fresh strawberries. It was about ninety-eight degrees, or it would have been idyllic.

After the picnic the girls began to play Old Bachelor, the feminist version of Old Maid. I bought the game thinking it was wonderful that the girls would not have to recoil in horror at the prospect of being left with the stereotypical old maid. My friend and I were dipping into her homemade salsa when I heard one of the girls ask Marybeth, my older daughter, about all the women on the cards. "Oh," she responded, "those are all the women the old bachelor didn't want." So much for circumventing the stereotypes.

10

As twilight entered the bowl and the sound and light engineers began testing the equipment, we began discussing the play. I can recap the plot in one long sentence: Good girl Sandy (a.k.a. Sandra Dee) meets bad boy Danny; Sandy decides to overwrite her good-girl image in order to be part of Danny's peer group. My friend noted that, although she likes the music very much, she doesn't like the message the play sends. In her words, "We get to watch Sandy cave in to peer pressure." As mothers of daughters we frequently lament the intense peer and cultural pressure our daughters face. I muttered my assent to her statement and then sat back as the play unfolded, mulling her comment over in my mind. And I'm now not sure, after some reflection, that I agree with her.

At the beginning of the play, Sandy is society's ultimate "good" girl. She swats Danny's hands away when he tries to touch her in "inappropriate" places. She admits that she has never had a drink of wine, and when the wilder girls, a.k.a. "The Pink Ladies," practically force her to drink, she retreats to the bathroom to worship the "porcelain goddess," what we called the commode when I was in high school and running around with a group much like The Pink Ladies. Sandy is "sweet" and "innocent" and "pure." Danny falls in love with her over the summer, but when she begins to attend Rydell High in the fall, she does not fit into his group of friends. Danny tries out for the track team in order to win the now cheerleading Sandy, but his constant smoking interferes with his track abilities. He isn't capable of changing, so Sandy does. In her swan song, "Goodbye to Sandra Dee," Sandy tells the "good" girl goodbye. She then appears in the next scene wearing tight-fitting black leather pants and a black halter with spaghetti straps. Her hair is frizzy, and she has on a great deal of makeup. She has become "hard." Danny lusts after her and literally drools; as she crooks her finger at him, he follows her on his hands and knees.

I have to wonder whether Sandy "caved in" or whether she gained power and control. At the beginning of the play Sandy is a quiet, inept, dependent human. By the conclusion, she is strong, forceful, and in control of the men. Granted, she is using her sexuality to control them, but, nevertheless, she is no longer played upon—she is a player. From a feminist perspective, she has found a voice and is not afraid to use it.

I remember this dichotomy from high school. I was a good Sandy in the eighth grade and to some extent my freshman year. And I was bored silly. I was bored with getting good grades, with spending Friday and Saturday nights playing Pac Man with my girlfriends. I wanted to taste the world. And I deliberately, like Sandy, remade myself. I stopped reading around people; I stopped trying in class. When I read, I did so secretly, mostly late at night (because I couldn't stop all the way). I started wearing skimpier clothing and running around with "wild" girls. I began to drink beer toward the end of my freshman year, and I kissed my first upperclassman at an all-night party when my friend's parents were out of town. And I had a blast. I learned to play "quarters," a drinking game, and we had parties on dirt roads outside of town. We met and built bonfires and roasted marshmallows beside the Missouri River on the sand dunes. We talked philosophy (does 3.2 beer and 5.0 beer differ that much?). But most of all we experienced life.

My friends, some from working-class families, were not afraid of much. My old friends from my "Sandra Dee" days wore their seat belts and watched movies together in their basements on Friday and Saturday nights. My new friends and I often drove across the border to Kansas, which had a drinking age of eighteen, when we were sixteen. We all had fake IDs, and we went into the bars and played pool, danced, and drank beer until the bars closed.

We did all the things that my parents were afraid we were doing. And I have almost no regrets. When I look back on that time in my life, I realize that, like "Sandra Dee," I said goodbye to my good-girl image because I instinctively knew that not only did good girls not have much fun, but that bad girls, in essence, had stronger voices. They knew how to use birth control, drive stick shifts, and shoot a beer bong. They also laughed loudly and did not tolerate girls who whined and giggled without cause. Probably we did not giggle period. And I don't think that I, in any way, caved in to peer pressure. If anything, I was rebelling against a society that told me that I was to be "sweet, kind, and virginal."

Ultimately, of course, I went on to college. There, I learned that I did not have to be either a "bad" girl or a "good" girl, and indeed, I attempted to figure out who I really was. Was my rebellious behavior part of me or merely a reaction to conservative parents and society in general? I fell in love with my college classes and drank in lectures and textbooks like we used to chug from the beer bong. I leapt into feminism with full speed and spent almost a year understanding the role that the dominant culture played in my own life and those around me. My understanding of feminism has evolved along with the choices I have made in my life, but it has remained a staying force throughout the passing years.

After *Grease* was over that summer night, we waited in the line of cars attempting to leave the parking lot and listened to our children attempt to sing "Look at Me, I'm Sandra Dee." I rolled down my window and shared with my friend my ruminations about the feminist aspects of the play. "I wish I had had more confidence in high school," I told her, "or a greater understanding of the dichotomy our society places before girls." She disagreed with my feminist interpretation of the play and leaned toward wanting her girls to adopt the role of "Sandra Dee," but I was, and am, not so sure. I was a "Pink Lady" that did not succumb to drugs or a house full of children with a husband who is either laid off or continually "hunting with the boys." The stereotype of what happens to "bad" girls is, I think, part of the dominant culture's attempt to keep women in their "place." My bad-girl training of facing fear, speaking up, and drinking a beer with the guys has helped me achieve more in my life than "sweet" and "innocent" ever have.

Obviously, in my ideal world there would be no "bad" or "good" girls but more choices to all young (and older) women. Educating women about the pressures of society along with the dangers of AIDS might help young girls understand the world that they must enter. But if the dichotomy between "good" and "bad" still exists when my girls enter young womanhood, and chances are that it will, I hope they refuse to drink—but I also hope they refuse to giggle.

• • •

Growing Up and Throwing Up

It has happened to them according to the true proverb,
"The dog turns back to its own vomit," and,
"The sow is washed only to wallow in the mud."
—*Peter 2:22*

I HAVE HAD MANY PASSIONS IN MY LIFE. WHEN I WAS IN THE sixth grade, I got a horse and loved to ride through the fields with my dad or by myself. We had Oklahoma Smoky, a dapple gray gelding, until I was twenty-six and rarely rode anymore. Nothing else was quite like the feeling of riding bareback in the countryside. It was good therapy for an adolescent girl to have a coarse mane to dry those tears from bad romances and lost friendships or just to hide a bad case of acne. I had bugged my dad for years to get a horse—not just a pony, like most girls dream of, but a real horse. I was shocked when he actually acquiesced. My dad and I had a famous time riding. Even though he had hay fever and asthma, he would go with me, sometimes donning a surgeon's mask to help keep out the irritants.

I was so passionate about riding that one snowy day I forded an ice-punctuated stream so high that it filled my boots with freezing water. I continued to ride with frostbitten toes for another hour until my dad realized how miserable I was. I wouldn't tell him because I didn't want to quit. He ended up taking off my boots and socks as we sat on a felled tree trunk, and he warmed my feet under his shirt on his 98.6 degree stomach and under his arms. I shook for two solid hours. When I finally got home and got warmed up, I threw up.

About the same time I was riding my horse every day, I was also very passionate about the CB radio. My handle, which is the radio equivalent of the "screen name" in the computer world, was "gray horse." I used to spend hours trying to reach people across town and across the world. I was so obsessed with it that I would sit out in the car in the freezing January weather with my coat and hat on and talk on the radio to faraway strangers. I remember being able to see my breath as I said my "ten-four"s. I got the flu after that episode and threw up for twelve hours.

CB was safer in those days than Internet chat rooms are today and never led to any face-to-face meetings. But I felt like I was exploring the big world out there and was trying to reach out and stay home all at the same time.

As I got older, sports became my haven. I loved basketball, tennis, track and field, and softball and played a sport every season. I worked hard, ran a lot, and was very competitive. Women's and girls' sports were just becoming acceptable and interesting at that time, and I didn't really notice that we had less funding, worse uniforms, or limited playing schedules compared to the boys. I had all the support I needed in the stands by my faithful parents and family.

I remember training for the first day of high school basketball. We ran several "thirty-second drills," and I was determined to be the fastest finisher every time. After winning a few too many, I promptly ran into the bathroom and threw up in the sink.

I had done well academically in high school. When I began college, I assumed that those good grades would continue for four more years without my having to study. So I "discovered" the world—which is a euphemism for partying a lot. I drank a lot of beer, stayed out too late, dated a lot, and got a different education than the one my parents paid for. And I threw up quite a few times. My grades were fine, but not the 4.0 I was expecting. At this point in my life, partying was not so much an obsession as it was a distraction.

When I worked as an engineer at twenty-four years of age, I had a boss who used to make inappropriate sexual comments and escalated his sexual harassment to the point of grabbing me by the shoulders, poking me in the ribs, or brushing his elbow against my breasts—conspicuously. It was too early in the legal history of sexual harassment for his behavior to be considered as warranting prosecution, but I did report him to the personnel department. I waited day after day for him to come in and punch me in the gut for getting him fired. Weeks went by, and the harassment was all I could think about. I drank a lot of Maalox, and even threw up once worrying about it. The boss was eventually fired, and I felt much better when he was gone.

Since I have become an adult, my obsessions have changed with the phases of my life. Dating used to be one of my obsessions; now caring for children is. Exploring and traveling used to be; now cocooning is. Romance and sex come and go, so to speak, but stability will always be one of my gods. And money. As a pastor, I have had to let go of that god, but it bites me from time to time.

I find it difficult to delineate what is interest, passion, obsession, or god. Usually when I am trying to convince myself that I'm not obsessed with something, it is too late. At times my obsession has been a new car. And then it is over. At times I had to have a husband. And then I was content to be single. At times I had to have a huge dish of chocolate ice cream before I went to bed every night. At other times I have been so obsessed with losing the postbaby weight that for several weeks I would run six miles a day and eat no fats. So when does a passion cross that line to becoming dangerous or even sinful? I never throw up anymore. I have no clear signal that I am overdoing things. How am I supposed to know?

Idolatry is a preacher's word, but it is an everyman and everywoman problem. We think we can't live without certain things. At times we can only think of one person, no matter how hard we try to shake it off. At other times we shut out our children in order to watch TV shows we think we must see.

Having an obsession is part of being human, true, but so is getting an infection. That doesn't make it good or right. Part of growing up is learning what you can live without. Part of growing up is learning balance. I learned how to deal with life's disappointments on those long trail rides when I sorted it all out. I learned balance on horseback—both literally and figuratively. I learned you can suffer in silence or speak up when you are hurt.

My obsessions have taught me that balance is better. But I would hate to be a woman without passion for something in my life. I just don't want to throw up anymore.

Pigtails to Perfume: Points to Ponder

1. Did you have a bad-girl image or a good-girl image growing up? How or when did you step out of that characterization?
2. How does playing a role help or hinder an individual's growth and development?
3. What messages do movies and TV programs communicate to young girls today?
4. Did any pivotal incidents during your teen years shape the woman you have become? What were they?
5. How could you help young women today grow up to be strong women of faith?
6. Read Joshua 2–6. Was Rahab "bad" or "good"?

Crossroads

Now faith is the assurance of things hoped for,
the conviction of things not seen.
—*Hebrews 11:1*

"WHAT MADE YOU DECIDE TO BECOME A MINISTER?" IS A QUES-
tion I get often from friends, acquaintances, and people who
can't fathom why a person would switch from the real world to
the church. "Why didn't you just keep your well-paying job and
do church work like most women?"

I never had a life-long dream to become a minister. I never
fantasized about preaching, helping people pick their way
through a marriage minefield, or holding hands with an elderly
woman on her deathbed. And yet, that is what I chose to do. I
was not motivated by a deep-seated desire to "help people" like
many pastors, psychologists, physicians, and social workers are.
In fact, I didn't think much of ministers, pastors, preachers, and
especially televangelists before my dramatic entrance into the
world of the church.

I grew up in a home where we said prayers before dinner, went
to Sunday school sporadically, and appreciated the goodness of creation regularly. But I wouldn't describe my childhood as particularly "religious." My grandmother had a Bible out on her coffee table
and attended a Presbyterian church faithfully. My parents both

went to the same Methodist college. But my family never pressured me to believe, much less join the profession of Christian leaders.

I had my career path all figured out. After graduation from college, I took the best of five job offers I had received to be a process engineer. I moved from Kansas to Pennsylvania without much of a second thought. I was excited about beginning my professional career, even though I didn't have a clue what I was doing. Designing things was easy on paper, but in the real world, what would happen if I misplaced a decimal point or forgot to convert to metric? It wouldn't be a letter grade at stake; it could be thousands of dollars, or worse.

So I entered the very male-dominated world of engineering and learned a bit from the school of hard hats. I traveled with gentlemen and with cads; I got advice from mentors and from lechers. I enjoyed my job, learned new things, and succeeded in my own little world. And quite unexpectedly, in that time of self-discovery bloomed an insatiable desire to know more about God. I had a Bible packed away in a box somewhere but wanted to know more, to read more, to understand more about my faith in Jesus. The ember of faith that I had was being fanned into a flame of yearning and desire to connect with God.

I sought out a Presbyterian church, went faithfully, joined the choir, helped a bit with the youth, and took the new members' class from the pastor. I joined shortly thereafter and became a part of a group of young people who were exploring their faith as well. This was a sustainable and happy life. I could work, travel, date around, drink beer on the weekends, go to church and choir, and feel balanced and satisfied in my life. I had it pretty well figured out. I was a grown-up.

But before too long, perhaps a bit too much beer and a bit too much dating around began to erode the road I was traveling. I made poor choices. I dated an atheist. I padded my expense account. I listened to my soon-to-be-fired coworker when he said, "Everyone usually puts an extra fifty dollars on their expenses for the trouble of having to travel out of town." There were no consequences, so why not?

It didn't take God long to figure out my Jekyll and Hyde game. One night, I prayed with some friends who were "worried" about me. They were far more experienced than I was in the world of religion, and they were far more vocal, especially during church. I'll never forget visiting their church and seeing, for the first time, people lift their hands, speak in tongues, and interrupt the preaching with shouts, songs, and comments of "amen" and "alleluia." They were decidedly not Presbyterian. We prayed together that evening, and I had a vision, not that I believed that people actually had visions. But I had one nevertheless.

That vision is as vivid today as it was when it happened fifteen years ago. What I saw was an open field, with mountains in the background. I was on a dirt road that wound around and headed toward those mountains. A way down the road was an intersection with a road going to the right and a road going to the left. At the intersection was a huge boulder; it was in the foreground and a bit to the left. On the road to the right was a man wearing a cloak and carrying what looked like a shepherd's crook. I thought it might be Moses or Jesus or one of those Bible-y characters. I moved on. At the end of the roads on the right and left sides were houses made out of caves—houses suspiciously like the one Fred Flintstone lives in.

My friends were amazed at the details of what I was describing. I wasn't in some trancelike state or on any drugs. I could open and close my eyes, and the picture was still there. Many times I interrupted my own narration with the comment "This is amazing!" They agreed.

I tried to travel down the road toward the mountains a bit but didn't see much. My friends suggested I go back to the man at the crossroad and try to see why he was there. So, I changed the focus of what I was seeing and looked more closely at the man. When I focused on him, I realized this was not Jesus or Moses or anything remotely good. He was not carrying a shepherd's crook; he was carrying a scythe. I focused on his face and saw a maniacal, evil, and twisted countenance that frightened the devil out of me. I wasn't sure what to do, so I prayed. They prayed. I don't even remember what I said, but it began to work. As we prayed, he moved toward Fred's house on the right and began to get smaller with each step and with each prayer. I was immediately relieved.

But when I stopped praying, the man loomed larger again. The feeling was oppressive, dangerous, and very frightening. We prayed more. He retreated and diminished.

We paused; he grew. We prayed without ceasing, and he finally became so small that he could fit under the door of the house. And the door closed tightly behind him. We kept praying, and the door was sewn shut. We prayed more, and the cave began to freeze over.

We stopped. We waited. When the cave began to heat up from the inside, we prayed more and more. We stopped focusing on the man, and kept praying for safety from this evil that grew each time we thought about it. We prayed in the name of

Jesus and for the mercy of God. And finally, a cold blast came from above, and the cave was frozen solid. And it stayed frozen.

We waited, and I watched. I looked up and opened and closed my eyes to be sure everything was the same. It was.

Once all was safe in this world of my vision, I explored the open field again. It was all the same, but with one slight difference. My perspective had changed. I was now on the other side of the crossroad. I had passed the intersection and the evil on the road, and now I had made some progress toward the mountains in the background.

There was peace. There was relief. And in the upper left hand corner of my peripheral vision was an open hole to the sky, an inky black sky dotted with shining stars. And in that opening, I could sense the face of Christ, looking into my world with unfathomable peace and joy.

And then the vision was over, and I went home. I was stunned. But even before I could figure out what it all meant, I was changed. Evil had lost part of its hold on me. I had been freed from something I didn't even understand and I knew, without question or concern, that God was real and had just extricated me from something evil. And my life was different. My perspective was different. My priorities were different.

I always knew I wanted to go to graduate school, probably in engineering or for an M.B.A., but one day my sister suggested seminary. Surprisingly, I was not repulsed by the idea. I looked at a seminary catalog and thought, "I want to take this class and that one and these two." I couldn't imagine taking "theories of vibration" or more physics. I wanted to soak up courses in theology, mission, church history, and Greek. I wanted to know it all. I wanted to know God more personally, more intimately, and more fully. I was giddy and euphoric and completely at peace with knowing God loved me.

Eight months later, I packed up all my belongings, moved to the West Coast, and began seminary. I didn't have a clue how I would pay for it, where I would live, or what I would end up doing. I only knew that it was what I wanted to do more than anything in my life. I knew God had called me closer, had put this fire in my heart to know more.

Sometimes I look back on that decision and wonder why I did it without knowing the cost. If I knew then what I know now, would I do it over again? Probably. Because at the time, the cost was inconsequential. Because I already had the reward. Because the calling was so strong. But a call to seminary is not necessarily a call to ministry. My frustrations come with the power struggles, the petty infighting, and the gossiping—all the things we humans do that we think a church should not.

My calling to be a minister in the church has been riddled with much more uncertainty than my calling to seminary ever was. To serve God was never a question. To serve people is another matter. At times I feel entirely satisfied, using every gift God has given me, affecting lives for Christ, building relationships, and mending marriages. At other times I get so frustrated with godly people doing ungodly things (myself included) that I want to walk away.

I continue to reevaluate my calling to the church and where God would have me serve. Some days I am surprised I can do anything at all, and other days I yearn to do more, sacrifice more, and give more. But not often.

I think most people's jobs are like that. Some days are great; others aren't. The problem with being at a crossroads, however, is figuring out what is pulling us to the right or to the left, forward or backward, and then moving ahead in faith. God has never spoken to me as clearly as on that evening in January of 1986. But because I felt it just that once, I know God is still guiding me. I long to travel that narrow path with the one who loves me and who led me through the valley of the shadow of death.

• • •

The Easter Penalty Box

After her great stories of sin, damnation, prophecy,
and revelation, the stories one reads casually in the average magazine
seem to be about love and roast beef.

—Alice Walker, "Beyond the Peacock: The Reconstruction of Flannery O'Connor"

WE WERE LATE FOR EASTER SUNDAY SERVICE. PUNISHMENT WAS swift and severe: we had to sit in the balcony. The balcony is the refuge for church members with small children who think that others won't notice when their kids run Hot Wheels up and down the backs of the chairs. I personally think the balcony is God's ironic way of sending me a couple of important FYI's.

First, my priorities need scrutiny. Why am I always late to church but never to class? Second, that vasectomy was a very good thing.

The balcony was packed; the church was pretty; the babies were wailing. The family behind us had a two-year-old and a three-year-old, and the mother was again pregnant. As the two-year-old hopped up and down in her chair singing the Barney song, I looked at my nine- and twelve-year-old daughters and sang with special meaning all the "alleluias." There was a time in my life when I couldn't imagine being without a little one to snuggle up with as I read *Go Dogs Go!* And now, looking back over the boxes of macaroni and cheese, the soccer games where screaming parents yelled for their kids to "go over to the weak side" and my daughter was the weak side, I feel peace and gratitude that we have made it this far, that we are, for the most part, whole.

As I listened to the Easter sermon, I thought about the mini-sermons I had preached in the classroom on the week leading up to Good Friday. We were reading Flannery O'Connor, the devout Catholic who infused Christianity into every short story she wrote. The problem with O'Connor's work, for most of us academicians, is that she writes so well. We are mostly humanitarians, we academicians. If you ask us about our religious beliefs, you will often get some sort of cross between Zen, Christianity, and New Age affirmations. We mostly don't do religion well; I, for sure, don't teach religion well. But I try. Teaching O'Connor always reminds me of the ultimate absurdity of my comfort zone in "try."

Literature is my passion, my driving force, the reason many days that I can walk into a classroom. I believe in the power of the written word, that the energy that rises from the page can change lives. It happened in mine; I have seen it work in the lives of others. I suppose the correct political stance would be to say that I teach for the students, but that would be a lie. I like the students, for the most part. But to be honest, after twelve years of teaching, they all sort of meld together. Some students stand out, of course: the woman who came to me trembling because, after reading Toni Morrison, she thought she might, after all, be racist; the young man with clear, bright eyes who told me that he wanted to be a writer. There are the students who come into my life and illuminate it. But mostly they don't. Mostly they whine about the reading, the writing, the analysis. They don't like Updike, Wharton is boring, and Hemingway is a drunk. But, classes have personalities, just like people, and the class to whom I taught O'Connor is a pretty good one. They have a sense of humor, a few students who truly read and seem to care about the characters they read about, and a couple of smart-asses who make all of us laugh.

But it wasn't me or the students during Wednesday's class that made it spectacular. It was one of those class periods when a certain theme takes hold and all the students wake up to see; their eyes drink in knowledge like the ground during a steady rain. We were reading O'Connor's "Everything That Rises Must Converge," a story about an intellectual young man who hates his mother because she lives by old southern standards all the while supporting his attempts to become a writer. The story drips with sarcasm and ultimately converges with the son's understanding of his own self-delusion and lack of compassion. So we talked about people who think they are better than others because of the color of their skin or the kind of car they drive or because (and I pointed to myself) they hold Ph.D.'s. My students were riveted. Words tumbled. They talked about a Greek system in which students thought they were better because they belonged to a certain "house." They talked about people who acted superior because they, or their parents, had piles of money. O'Connor's vision of Christianity entered my classroom and held my students spellbound for fifty minutes. As they walked out, one of the students came over to me and said awkwardly, "Well, um, thanks." And I said, "You're welcome." But the thanks, of course, go to O'Connor.

What is truly cool (my students have entered my vocabulary) is that Flannery O'Connor fought lupus from her early twenties until she died at the age of thirty-nine. She watched her father suffer from this disease throughout her childhood, and then she spent her adult life writing through the disease that finished her off, as it did her father. She didn't have time for pleasantries. Her writing is funny and grotesque and fierce. And I consider it a rare gift to be paid for the pleasure of discussing her work, her vision. She believed that, overall, most of us are pretty rotten. We are selfish, arrogant, and blind to gratitude. So O'Connor created characters just like us, and then she had them meet with some type of awful violence. The violence usually forces the characters to see the world from a different place (such as hanging upside down from a bull's horn that has just gored through a character's stomach), and that revelation ultimately provides the saving grace—the character understands his or her actions and repents.

O'Connor most often attacks the intellectuals, the outwardly pious, the hypocrites. She goes after those who think they are just a little bit better than others because their kitchen floor is cleaner or their children's noses are wiped or they lead good "Christian" lives. I think of her, limping on her crutches around her southern farmhouse, and I wish I could have a cup of tea with her. I wish I could tell her about my students and our class and how her work lit up a whole lot of lives for just a few minutes.

Many days, weeks even, I struggle with my faith. When my friend Teri died, when I recently discovered that my sister's mammogram came back with a spot, I, like Job, felt like shouting, "Hey, are you napping up there? 'Cause we're in a lot of trouble down here." I know that bad things happen to good people; I know all the clichés. But one's feeling of the presence of God must go beyond that. On good days, I feel that presence like a shy child's smile. On the bad days, I reach for Hemingway and, strangely, find comfort there. Hemingway was an atheist, but his stories are filled with characters who follow Christian principles in spite of their unbelief. Nick Adams, one of his main characters in a collection of short stories, comes back from World War I shaky and psychologically damaged. He goes fishing, and nature brings him slowly but surely back to a place where he can begin to balance the horrors of war and the guilt for surviving with the natural beauty of the river and the art of fishing. Nick may not have proclaimed himself a Christian, but regardless of Hemingway's atheist leanings, I find God everywhere in "The Big Two-Hearted River." I believe that a person cannot write well without a deep love of people; Hemingway and O'Connor demonstrate their profound love for humans, flawed and pathetic though we often are, with majesty and grace.

So, on this Easter, sitting in the penalty box that is the balcony, I thank God for my family, the ages of my children, and the fact that I have a consuming and sustaining passion for literature and the people who write it. I am so grateful for Flannery O'Connor and her work, for Hemingway, a testament to both literature and religion that the two are not irreconcilable. And on this beautiful day in April I think that perhaps nothing is impossible; perhaps over time my faith will find such solidity that there will be no more days of doubt, of frustration. In the meantime, I will try to get myself to the church on time.

• • •

Calling the Wild: Points to Ponder

1. What are you grateful for? Does this gratitude inform your work life? If so, how?
2. Do you like what you do? If not, how might you change that?
3. Has your faith in God influenced your career decision? If so, how?
4. What do you feel passionate about in your life? How do you act on that passion?
5. Does God really give people visions and speak to them through books? How do we know it is God and not a fantasy or daydream?
6. Has any passage of Scripture been useful to you in determining what God has gifted you to do in your vocation? Which one?
7. Read Deuteronomy 6:4-9. How might you follow the instructions found there?

Of Wedding Rings and Sailing Ships

For one thing, the Héloïses and Abelards,
the Pelléases and Mélisandes,
do not get married and stay married forty years.

—*Madeleine L'Engle,* Two-Part Invention

SO THE TRUTH OF THE MATTER IS THAT I DON'T KNOW OF ANY extraordinarily successful marriages that also involve children— older children, I mean (babies don't count). I know quite a few of the academic sort who marry and have lovely marriages, but generally they do not have children. Rather, they evolve into a quaint and usually gentle couple who do nice things for each other. Or they divorce. But happily married couples with children seem to appear to me only in Disney films, and we usually don't see Cinderella washing Prince Charming's underwear. Now, I was not a stupid kid. I noticed these things. My parents' marriage was not unhappy, but it certainly was not the kind of marriage that I wanted. My friends' parents, as far as I could tell, had the same kind of marriage my parents had. And the divorced stepparent thing was even worse. They called each other gross nicknames and made out in front of the kids. Definitely not going there.

So when Wayne and I had been dating for five years and our

parents knew we were quasi living together, they began to apply pressure. I liked our life the way it was. We each had our own place, our own peanut-butter jar, and things worked well. Why mess it up? Wayne sided with the parents. He wanted commitment. He wanted to see me when he woke up. He wanted (well, let's be honest) free sex and free laundry service.

So, I suggested a partnership contract. I wanted to be, not the traditional husband and wife, but legal, equal partners in life. I argued the odds. What are our chances, I pleaded, to make it when we don't know any marrieds with kids who have the kind of relationship we want? I told him I wasn't going to be happy with anything less than fifty-fifty sharing of household and eventual childcare duties. He promised me that wouldn't be a problem.

We married.

He lied.

So the first time Wayne called me from work and said that he was going to be late because he was going out with the guys and I already had supper ready (cooking disappeared fast from the deal), I was fine. Then it was small things. Could I pick up his dry cleaning? Could I call the airlines about a flight to Chicago? Didn't we just have spaghetti a few nights ago? After about three months of marriage, I blew. I melodramatically pulled off my wedding rings, called him a liar and a scamp (well, maybe something a bit stronger), and threw the rings at him with all my might.

He picked the rings up out of the sofa cushions. Apologized. Told me he would be better. I believed, he tenderly put the rings back on my finger, and we made up in, to use the euphemism, royal fashion.

The next ring-throwing event came about a year later. We now had a baby. Wayne had been traveling for a week, and when he walked in the door, I was feeding the baby applesauce. He looked at us both, hung up his coat, and said absently, "So how much money did you spend this week?" The first spoonful of applesauce hit the side of his face, the second, his tie. As I began pelting his expensive suit, shoes, and hair with applesauce, he began dodging. Applesauce hit the sofa, the walls, and the carpet. The rings followed. I packed the diaper bag, picked up the baby, and roared off to a motel.

He picked the rings up out of the applesauce. Apologized. Told me he would be better. I believed, he tenderly put the rings back on my finger, and we made up in, to use the euphemism, royal fashion.

The next Christmas when the baby was two we quarreled. He was busy at work; he didn't have time to buy Christmas presents. I was teaching and taking classes only three days a week, and surely I could find time to buy the presents. The rings disappeared into the tree. A shakedown after he apologized and we made up didn't even make the rings appear. "I think," he said, "you'd better stop wearing them." I nodded. We later found them under the tree skirt.

And it made perfect sense to me. Wayne wore his wedding ring because our marriage worked very well for him. I was a good mother, a scrupulous housecleaner, and carried on a pretty good conversation at parties. My dreams of marriage, however, were shattered. I realized that my husband was never going to become a fifty-fifty father or husband. His chosen profession demanded that he work fifty to sixty hours a week, and that simply didn't leave time enough for the kind of partnership I had imagined and he had promised.

But we had this darling little girl, we had a beautiful home, and I was pregnant again. We figured out some compromises. He would buy and send all birthday/wedding/sympathy cards and presents for his extended family, and I would do mine. I would not pick up dry cleaning, but I would do laundry. I undoubtedly did 90 percent of the housework, and when my frustration would become too unmanageable, I would call him at work and tell him I couldn't do it anymore. I would beg for us to join the Peace Corps. Those were resentment days. We called it the "R" word. If I was grouchy, he would say, "Is it the R-factor?" and I would say yes or no depending. We were settling. I felt it.

But the Christmas before Erin was born, Wayne asked if I thought I could wear a ring if he got me one just like his—a plain silver band, inexpensive, to symbolize our new understanding that fifty-fifty didn't mean just doing the laundry. He worked hard so that we could have a nice home, car, and an occasional trip to Breckinridge. His life wasn't all lunch at the Savoy Grill. I understood, at least partially. I said I'd try.

I lasted until June when my friend Kelly got married. I was a bridesmaid. At the reception, Wayne and I were sitting across the table from each other when I heard a friend ask Wayne something about married life. I was talking to another woman at the table and so pretended not to hear when Wayne said it was great, that he loved it. I don't know now what I wanted to hear. Probably something about marriage being an equal partnership. Probably something about the fact that I was not his "wife," but a person. I threw the ring. He saw me throw it. It landed in a glass of beer next to the groom, and I had to laugh. I hoped he would leave it; a glass of beer seemed a fitting place for it to finally rest. My accountant significant other, however, politely asked the guy for his beer, fished the ring out, and put it in his pocket. "I think," he said on the way home, "that we better give up on the wedding rings."

And so I haven't worn a wedding ring for almost ten years. In that time I have seen couples marry, divorce, and remarry. Many of them asked why I didn't wear a ring. Many were skeptical, though they laughed at the wedding ring story. It is funny, but it is also sad because I truly thought we could beat the system. I thought we could preserve our edge, hedge ourselves against resentment, boredom, and annoyance as long as we did not engage in the overt symbols of marriage. We had a very small plain wedding. My first wedding rings were antiques we bought in a dusty shop. I never referred to Wayne as my husband.

It didn't matter. I planned a marriage that could not exist in the world in which we live. And, in an odd way, my inability to wear a wedding ring still speaks to that hope, that hope that somehow, somewhere, we have kept that spark alive. Perhaps after the children are grown, perhaps after the dishes have been done and the dog has been walked, we might remember our relationship at its best and brightest: the nights we sat and talked until two in the morning about what kind of parents we wanted to be, the parties where we were the first on the dance floor and the last to leave, the times when our eyes would meet across a room and we couldn't wait to be alone.

Sometimes now we go whole weeks without anything to

remind me that we aren't two people who have agreed, for the children's sake, to be kind to one another. Or at least civil. And it's neither of our faults, nor is it a problem that can be solved by a two-page article in *Good Housekeeping* reminding us to "nurture each other." It is difficult when both of us work and have children in activities and siblings and friends and a coworker with cancer to say, "Hi, honey, how was your day?" Some days it is difficult to even care.

I look, now and then, at my left hand, and I know that my bare finger is a testament to a relationship that was, and I hope will one day be again, the best thing that ever happened to me.

• • •

Prince Charming

Love is patient; love is kind; love is not envious or boastful or arrogant or rude. It does not insist on its own way; it is not irritable or resentful; it does not rejoice in wrongdoing, but rejoices in the truth. It bears all things, believes all things, hopes all things, endures all things.

Love never ends. But as for prophecies, they will come to an end; as for tongues, they will cease; as for knowledge, it will come to an end. For we know only in part, and we prophesy only in part; but when the complete comes, the partial will come to an end. When I was a child, I spoke like a child, I thought like a child, I reasoned like a child; when I became an adult, I put an end to childish ways. For now we see in a mirror, dimly, but then we will see face to face. Now I know only in part; then I will know fully, even as I have been fully known. And now faith, hope, and love abide, these three; and the greatest of these is love.

—*1 Corinthians 13:4-13*

I THOUGHT I'D NEVER GET MARRIED. THROUGH COLLEGE, MY first job, and seminary I didn't see it happening. At twenty and twenty-four, I began to wonder. At twenty-six and twenty-seven, I began to worry. I dated and had a great time, fell in and out of love, and had a few near misses, one complete-with-ring proposal and two "I want to marry you" discussions that never got off the ground.

Part of me wanted perfection. Part of me wanted good looks. Part of me wanted the big bucks. But mostly I just wanted a soul mate. I wanted to marry a stable, handsome, winsome Christian man who enjoyed life, was responsible, and wanted children. It would never happen.

Or so I thought. The first time I remember seeing Dan, he was playing his guitar for a group of students at a Presbyterian gathering in a seminary classroom. He and I were students in the same seminary and took a class together that summer. I remember thinking when I saw him singing and strumming, "I wonder if that is the man I will marry?" Kind of a strange thought, but it did stick with me. Funny, I happened to be dating someone else at the time.

Soon, Dan and I courted; we studied; we laughed. We came to know the Bible, but not each other in a biblical sense. I visited his family; he visited mine. We whispered in the library and talked theology over sandwiches. I wasn't convinced I would or should marry him, but we did mull it over.

And then Dan surprised me—in grand style. I was taking a youth group of ninety kids from L.A. to Utah for a church ski trip. I was one of several adult leaders who chaperoned, led Bible study, sang, prayed, and skied with the kids. One of the other adult leaders persuaded me to go out and meet a friend in the parking lot who was there to visit. I didn't have time for that. I had just spent the day skiing, was in dire need of a shower, had hat hair, and had to prepare that evening's events. But he wouldn't relent. So, I reluctantly agreed to meet his pesky friend and then go about my business.

When we walked to the parking lot, I noticed the kids were hovering around, nonchalantly watching us. Some were giggly; some were hiding. I ignored them and ran down the list of things I had to do in my mind.

When we reached the parking lot, there was Dan. He was dressed as Prince Charming from head to toe, with a white vest with a yellow cross on it, a white cape draped across his shoulders and tied with a white rope. He was standing beside a horse-drawn carriage. Did I mention I had hat hair and hadn't showered yet that day?

He escorted me into the carriage, and we drove away, along the pine needle path and through the forest. On the ride, he presented me with a ring, encased in a crystal box that was sewn onto a white satin pillow. He said, "I love you and want to spend the rest of my life with you. Will you marry me?" I didn't speak. Long pause.

"Well?" he asked.

This was the moment I had been waiting for, and fearing. Was he "the one"? Was this the right decision? Was this going to work? I wasn't quite ready, and yet I wanted to say yes.

"Well?" he said, this time a little concerned.

"Yes, yes, a thousand times yes!" was my reply. He seemed quite relieved.

I didn't realize he had called my parents earlier that week to "ask for my hand." When I called them that evening to give them the good news, they already knew about it. They had given their blessing and said the decision was up to me.

Prince Charming wasn't what I expected—at least not in a proposal of marriage. I had been in and out of love enough to know that some things aren't what they are cracked up to be. It had never been a fantasy of mine to be whisked away by a rescuer, to be a damsel in distress. It may have been his fantasy to be Prince Charming, but not mine. And yet there was something deeply satisfying about it: to have a "suitor" call my parents, surprise me with not only his flight to Utah on a student's budget but a costume, horse-drawn carriage, and the secret accomplices in my youth group putting up the ruse. I was impressed.

Our marriage has unfolded throughout the years. What appeared from the proposal to be a "traditional" relationship has evolved into one of the most equitable marriages I have seen. We share chores, responsibilities, childcare, finances, career opportunities, cooking, yard work, and just about anything else that comes up. But it has taken a while to get to this point.

After the birth of our third child, when I was feeling overwhelmed by the exponential growth of responsibility, we sat on our back deck, and I announced, "This isn't working for me. This is too much work. You need to do more stuff." He was stunned. He did, after all, do a lot already. But there was a lot more to do. And, over the course of a few weeks and in the past few years, he has picked up more and more of the load. Whoever thinks of it on Thursday evening puts the first load of laundry in (usually me). Whoever walks by the washer next advances the laundry to the dryer (usually him). Whoever wants to watch the game on TV folds the clothes (usually him). I pick up toys, magazines, books, and miscellany. I vacuum, and I order the kids to dust. He cleans the bathrooms, takes out the trash, prepares sack lunches every weekday morning, cooks dinner about half the time, and cleans the kitchen on the nights I cook. I tidy, make beds (sometimes), clean the kids' rooms and the closets, buy almost all their clothes, and usually do the grocery shopping. I clip tiny fingernails; he keeps the vehicles running and clean. I do the big spring-cleaning projects, and he asks what he can do to help.

All in all, it is a great arrangement. Oh, sure, at times I wish he wouldn't ask, "What needs to be done in the house?" I wish he'd just do it. When I tell my girlfriends this, they look at me like I'm nuts. I've learned most husbands don't do the things mine does. At other times I think he cleaned the bathroom in the dark because as soon as I turn on the light, I can see the streaks and spots he missed and dirty towels that long for the hamper. Having two boys with lousy aim makes that job a real tummy turner. But for the most part, we share all that we can. Having two churches and three small children is a huge job.

One of my biggest frustrations is that Dan has bought into the urban myth that when a wife asks her husband, "Am I fat?" or "Should I get my hair cut?" it is an invitation to battle. His response is always guarded. He feels there is no right answer. But I continually point out to him that I have never once pounced on him for his answer. I really just want an opinion. I may disregard it, or I may decide he's right. But he won't give me a clear answer. He's listened to too many comedians who say that a man's best bet in this scenario is to feign a bowel obstruction. I get madder that he won't answer me than I would if he said I needed to drop about twenty pounds and get a face-lift instead of a haircut.

We bicker. I nag. He shuts down. But not very often. We have learned each other's strengths and weaknesses and how to work through them. Even after I said yes, I wasn't sure I could commit. Now I can't think of any reason why I ever doubted.

The Prince Charming that I envisioned in my fantasy wasn't one with a white cape or horse-drawn carriage. He was one who would love me, respect me, and be great fun in the sack. He would cuddle the kids and kill the mice. He would be smart and witty and would enjoy my family. He would be responsible, but not boring. He would be independent, yet need me. He would be funny, but not embarrassing. And he would want the best for me in my career, hopes, and dreams.

The reality isn't exactly what I fantasized about but is certainly closer than I thought it would be. And the relationship is even better because we've worked together to make it so.

Happily Ever After: Points to Ponder

1. When you were younger, what was your fantasy of marriage?

2. How has your perspective on marriage changed? What have been your most encouraging and disappointing realizations?

3. Have you ever been angry enough to contemplate severing a close relationship (if married, to contemplate divorce)? If so, what were the circumstances?

4. How has choosing to have children (or not) changed your personal relationships or your marriage?

5. What can you do to make your personal relationships better, happier, and more equitable?

6. When you read 1 Corinthians 13, can you see strengths and weaknesses in your own relationships? What are the strengths? What are the weaknesses?

You Can't Take a Joke

Therefore God gave them up in the lusts of their hearts to impurity, to the degrading of their bodies among themselves, because they exchanged the truth about God for a lie and worshiped and served the creature rather than the Creator, who is blessed forever! Amen.

—*Romans 1:24-25*

WHEN I GRADUATED FROM COLLEGE AND TOOK MY FIRST JOB as an engineer, I learned a lot about all those things you discover when you go to the "school of hard knocks." I learned what a real deadline was, not one imposed by my teacher. I learned that millions of dollars could be at stake if you were to take too long on a construction project—thousands of dollars per day for each day you ran behind. I learned how wonderful it is to have a secretary to facilitate your job. I could have used a secretary in college.

But one of the more difficult lessons I learned after college was how to deal with men. Before this time, I had dealt with many men, of course, as teacher, father, boyfriend, classmate, and coach. And most of the men I knew were great guys. My own brother was a great example to me of how to be a friend and still be "all guy." He led me through the maze of high school relationships and introduced me to his friends—if they were good enough. I would avoid the men out there whom I could identify as jerks, and I was fortunate enough not to have any bullies or abusers in my world.

But when I went to work at a male-dominated workplace, where the men were the engineers and the women were the secretaries and I was the exception, I learned that a lot of men did not want me there. They preferred me to be out of their working environment altogether. And if that couldn't happen, they wanted sex.

I worked with many admirable and wonderful men. But they are not the ones I remember. I remember the ones who would constantly harass me and make sexual innuendos and hint of times we could have together if only we could "get naked." At twenty-two, my response ranged from being flattered to being frightened. Most of the "guys" were just making "guy" comments out of fun. And I found some of these comments amusing. Many comments were harmless to me as an individual because I could ignore or discount them. I didn't perceive it as a particularly sex-charged environment because I was twenty-two, and most of the guys in college speak that way to women. The regular guys weren't the problem.

To have a boss or the boss's boss make hints that he is so very lonely and his wife is so terribly inept at understanding him and then say, "Don't you need a nice back rub after a long day? You're so witty, so beautiful, so understanding," really makes an impression—usually a very awkward one. One boss would come up behind me as I was working at the drafting table and tickle me in the ribs. He liked to hear me scream, he said, as he startled me. One day, on a business trip together, he placed his hand around my calf and scrunched down my panty hose and said, "That's

what my wife's ankles look like without her hose on." Weird.
Then, when we were working through dinner at a hotel on a
long project, he grabbed me around the shoulders, threw me on
the bed, and jumped on top of me. I was so surprised and disgusted I yelled for him to get off me. He got up, threw his head
back, laughed, and said, "You looked like you really believed I
would try something! You're so funny." I walked out.

As I accused, he rebuffed. "You can't take a joke," he said, "I
was just kidding." I reported him, waited a few months in
agony for him to get the ax and then take it out on me. He was
eventually fired for a number of unethical deeds. I was relieved
when he went, hoping I'd never see him again.

I wish I could say that was the last episode of sexual harassment I've endured, but it wasn't. The difference is that I'm more
attuned to other people's words and am better able now to distinguish appropriate comments from inappropriate ones. Society and the workplace have changed some as well, and
personnel policies are much less tolerant of the kinds of situations I found myself in at my first job.

I would have hoped that working in the church would mean
that I am now safe from those kinds of comments and sugges-
tive body language. But that is not the case. One member likes
to give all the church ladies hugs, but seems to plant his hand a
little too high or a little too low each time. One man asks me
for counseling to improve his sex life, "Where should I touch
my wife to get her interested in sex?" I can now deflect him by
saying, "Her heart."

But the most difficult parishioner I have ever dealt with surprised me. He was one of the most helpful, useful, friendly men

I'd met. But he would make comments like "I heard a rumor that you and I were having an affair," or "I'm glad to see you are wearing a skirt today. There's a light bulb that needs to be changed on the ceiling of the office." However, the one that made me the maddest was "You should do baptisms like the Baptists do. Get in the water and get all wet. And you could wear a see-through white T-shirt, and then everyone would want to get baptized."

I have learned that no place offers complete freedom from other people's sexual perversion. I am not safe in the office or the church, the bar or college. But I have learned to deal appropriately with men's advances. Sometimes I ignore them, and sometimes I turn them in. Fortunately for all of us, more people in leadership today will speak out against sexual harassment of any kind than would leaders fifteen years ago.

I don't like the feeling of needing to be rescued, but I know I need society's help in changing norms. Fewer men will now say, "You can't take a joke" than fifteen years ago, but still too many men think their comments are harmless.

• • •

Independence Day, 2000

Why d[o] men drink wine and women water?

—*Virginia Woolf*, A Room of One's Own

SO YESTERDAY WAS THE FOURTH OF JULY, AND MY FATHER AND I sat on my sister's deck and had our usual Independence Day talk. We have the talk every year on this day, and we both look forward to it. It begins as a sort of "state of the world" discussion but soon moves into the central argument that began when I was twelve years old: the implications of gender roles in society (I should say the society with which my father and I identify: Midwestern, white, upper middle class).

My father belongs to the generation that Tom Brokaw calls the "Greatest." I don't know whether I agree or disagree with this label, but what I do know is that my mother and father's generation had fairly rigid boundaries for male and female behavior. I also know that many couples did not conform to the June and Ward Cleaver stereotypes, but my parents certainly did. So at the presumptuous age of twelve, I said to my father as my mother rushed to get him yet another glass of iced tea, "Why can't you get your own iced tea?" He stopped in the middle of buttering his bread and looked at me quizzically. "Why can't you get your own iced tea?" I repeated. He gave me a look that I have since privately referred to as "The Look." This is the look people give me and others when we ask seemingly innocent questions that, in no small way, threaten to overturn the social order.

I do not even remember his response; I only recall his look, which was one of fear swiftly replaced by anger and then sarcasm. This interpretation is perhaps too complex to be attributed to me as a twelve-year-old. I suppose in the years following I have learned to identify and recognize The Look in such a way that I understand it now in a way that I could not have then. I imagine that he told me that when I started earning a living, then I could tell him how to run his house and so on.

The following year my father bought my mother a retail

store, and she went to work full-time managing the E&M Shoppe. She still fetched his iced tea. "So Mom's earning a living now. Why does she still have to get your iced tea?" I inquired at some point the following year. What ensued was an argumentative debate about biological and sociological roles that lasted until almost midnight and off and on for the next twenty and continuing years. We dredge up the old argument on the Fourth of July specifically as part of our evaluation of the evolution of the changing society around us. The rest of our family—husband, wife, siblings, children, grandchildren—leave immediately.

"You're having a bad year," my father said this Independence Day. "Hillary's not doing so well in New York. I guess people don't like the women libbers after all."

"It's not about the feminist issue," I tell him. "Hillary has played too many sides of the fence. Nobody trusts her."

"Well, I think women are in even worse shape this year than last. Divorce rates are still up. The paper says that women and children are in even more poverty than ever before. You women did yourselves an injustice when you went to work and said you were going to make the living. Now the man doesn't have to do anything. He doesn't have the pressure of making a living for his family, and he still gets everything else. You women are turning yourselves into pretzels, and for what?"

I can't argue with him on the Superwoman problem. The majority of women I know who work full-time are exhausted. And most women I know who stay home full-time are depressed or over-involved in their children's social lives. "But at least we have options now," I tell him. "At least we don't devote our whole lives to washing some man's underwear and then have him trade us in for a new model when we are at an age when it's difficult to start over."

He nods. Point for me. "But that didn't happen as often as you think," he said. "Most of the time people in my generation stayed married. We knew what it meant to be a man or a woman. Your generation let men off the hook. They don't have to do anything, really. I think women were better off when they stayed home."

"They were in a padded cage, Dad." I gesture with my arms, becoming more emphatic. "At least I choose to be a pretzel. At least it was my choice to get married, to choose a career where I could work part-time and now full-time. I don't sit home and wait to see if my husband likes my pot roast. That would be a living hell. As history tells us, separate isn't always equal."

He grins, "Your mother makes an excellent pot roast."

"So you stay home and make pot roast and wait with anticipation to see if someone will compliment it so you can feel validated," I snort at the picture.

"Validated, hell. Every person makes his or her own happiness. I could be happy staying home, or I could be happy working. It's all a mind-set."

I take this ball and dribble it down the court. "Sure it's all a mind-set. Men got to set up the rules. For instance, who decided that women had to do laundry while men mowed the yard? The yard doesn't even have to be mowed in the winter for God's sake."

"So change the rules then. Get all the women libbers together and change the world. In my experience women fight every time they get together, so I don't think I'll worry too fast."

"We are changing the world," I tell him. "Whether you like

it or not, my daughters will not think that their goal in life is to marry a man and assume his identity. They know that they have to make a life and have a career of their own. We are changing the world one daughter at a time."

"I don't see the world tumbling down anytime soon," he said as we were summoned to the table where my sister was placing grilled hot dogs and hamburgers. He turned to go into the house to use the rest room before we ate.

"Dad," I called. He turned. "Will you bring me a glass of iced tea when you come out?"

He almost smiled. "I'll think about it," he said as he closed the door.

Independence is a great gift to have. But often it must be won.

• • •

Women's Work: Points to Ponder

1. Approximately one in four college-aged women will be raped during her four years as an undergraduate. Why do you think violence toward women is at an all-time high?

2. Are you frustrated by people's views of you or your career? How do you deal with the frustration and with them?

3. What barriers exist in society that still impede women's progress to be perceived as equals with men?

4. How have you contributed to these barriers? How have you challenged them?

5. What world do you imagine for your great-granddaughters?

6. Read Proverbs 31:10-31. Does this support or challenge the stereotype of women's work?

Sex and the Jiggle Factor

…two by two in the ark of the ache of it.
—*Denise Levertov, "The Ache of Marriage"*

A FEW YEARS AGO, A NEIGHBOR OF MINE CAME OVER TO HAVE coffee. "Guess what he wants now?" she asked (the "he" being her husband). "He wants me to lose twenty pounds. He told me that he would pay me a hundred dollars for every pound I lose." I shook my head. "You know what I told him?" I shook my head again. "I told him that when I wake up next to Tom Cruise, then I'll worry about losing twenty pounds." I laughed, she laughed, and we launched into how much Christmas shopping she had left. But it reminded me how important our spouses are to us, body and soul.

What I like most about sex is the vulnerability inherent in the act. Most of the time, at least in modern culture, people seem to wear masks. We pretend to be happy when we are not, fine when we ache inside. We mask our loneliness in Chanel suits and Bandolino pumps; we hide emptiness in the immaculate seats of our leather interiors or in the crumpled-up McDonald's bags that line our car floors. We attempt to project an image we want to be, or at least want others to see. We might wear Control Top pantyhose and Wonderbras, but underneath, in our skin, we know that for the most part, we jiggle.

Sex is the underneath part.

Sex is, in all honesty, a completely unaesthetic act. Advertisers attempt to convince us that sexual intercourse is beautiful. They often showcase lovely people in skimpy clothes and intimate that these people are going to engage in "cool" sex. But the bottom line is that sex isn't cool. It's often bumpy and lumpy and awkward. I smile as I think of buttons that won't open, sheets that get tangled, kids that knock at the most inopportune time. But it is real. Skin against skin, mouth against mouth, the body can't be masked, shielded. In the act of sex, we are, man and woman, vulnerable, emotionally at risk.

Because few people are comfortable with vulnerability, we surround sex with silly meanings. Society talks easily about multiple orgasms and "mile high" clubs in an attempt to gain control over the act; we label positions and zones in order to make sex complex and perhaps more dignified. But sex isn't about dignity, as any high schooler caught by police on a seemingly deserted road with his hand up his girlfriend's blouse can tell you. Sex is about getting underneath—underneath the clothes—but, more importantly, removing the facade that keeps us from truly knowing another person.

In one of my favorite novels, *A Tree Grows in Brooklyn*, Aunt Sissy declares, "If the sex is good, the marriage is good." I did not understand this emphasis when I read the book at age eleven, but now I think she definitely has a point (no pun intended). Or maybe the pun was intended. Even when I try to talk seriously about sex, I find humor in every other word I attempt to type. When my best friend in third grade whispered to me what sex really was, I was incredulous. She neglected to mention the erection part, and I imagined that sex occurred with a person at opposite ends of the bed pulling at each other's ankles to accomplish the feat. I thought it was so silly, so, well …ridiculous. And justifiably so.

I like to think that sex was designed to be silly, ridiculous, and awkward in order to remind us that our posturing will ultimately fail. At the moment many of us would like to be invincible, we are forced to come to one another in vulnerability. I think some of the most intimate moments in my marriage have come after sex, when the masks have fallen. I have stopped holding in my tummy and hoping that my hair is falling becomingly across my face. It is usually in that quiet, nonlinear time that we talk about real stuff. Or, if life is good, we giggle like little kids over stupid things. If our relationship is in a bad stint, and there have been those times, then we are silent—and that is one of the most awful silences I know.

Sex almost always reminds me that, much as I might not like to admit it, I am part of the world that drools, eats garlic, and often forgets to shave. I remember in college when women in my sorority would ogle men in soap operas and discuss which one they would marry if they could. I also remember when a friend of mine, a year or two after she married, reported that she was no longer "in love" with her husband but rather "loved" him. She noted that after she saw her spouse get out of the shower day after day, he just was not that exciting anymore. I understand. I dated my husband for five years before we married, and we have been married quite awhile. I tell him when he has food stuck between his teeth, and he notes the runs in my pantyhose. On some days we coordinate our family's schedule like drill sergeants. Some nights he comes home exhausted and falls asleep reading the newspaper after dinner. I wonder where the young boy who brought me roses and kissed my cheek so gently on our first date went. I worry about losing our passion, our connectedness. I wonder if, indeed, I know this man at all.

But, now and then, if I'm lucky, I realize that he's still the same—underneath.

• • •

Peaks and Valleys

How beautiful you are, my love,
   how very beautiful!
Your eyes are doves
   behind your veil.
Your hair is like a flock of goats,
   moving down the slopes of Gilead.

—*Song of Solomon 4:1*

"HE'S MAD AT ME AGAIN BECAUSE HE DIDN'T GET ANY THIS morning." So begins yet another phone conversation with my girlfriend about her husband and their sex life. From time to time we compare notes about sex. I revel in the honesty we can share with each other, the inside jokes about libido, and the compassion we have for one another's seasons of no passion.

We marvel together about "the way it used to be." "Remember when you were in love, in lust, and intertwined?" she asks me. "Vaguely," I answer. She has two children; I have three. We talk about the way we used to initiate, the way we used to pine for our men, and the way we used to be spontaneous.

And then we bred. After having a baby hang on your breast to nurse, lugging him or her in your arms, and having a toddler pull on your baby-food-stained sweatpants all day, you don't feel much like "giving it up." You've been giving all day. You don't need one more person asking you for one more thing—especially if it might lead to more babies.

As my girlfriend and I experienced that preschooler and baby phase together, we learned that what we felt, or didn't want to feel, was normal. Understanding this, I could more easily tell my husband, without feeling guilty, how I really felt about having sex. I'm not saying I particularly enjoyed having my libido shut down by toddlers, but at least I wasn't castigating myself for being unavailable.

My husband was surprisingly understanding and, perhaps, frustrated. But it didn't take him long to get over it and think maybe he'd ask again in a month or so.

Those were the baby years. Then an amazing thing happened on the way to the bedroom. Both of us, my girlfriend and I, at different times due to the different ages of our children, got it back. The need, the want, and the desire all came flooding back as if we had found long-lost friends in the airport and couldn't believe they were back in our arms after such a long separation.

She confessed a particularly interesting tryst in her walk-in closet. I marveled. I told her about the week we were 5 for 7. She applauded. But she also made me swear not to tell her husband that couples our age still did that.

I remember one day I started to tell her a particularly interesting tidbit about our recent success, and she burst into tears.

She and her husband had been arguing over the frequency of sex in their household. In that particular season of life, he was needy, and she was distracted. I listened as she told about her frustrations, and his.

A few weeks later, when things were going better for her, she asked me, "You were getting ready to tell me something very interesting that day I was in tears. I've been meaning to ask you what it was about." So I told her. Even when she wasn't enjoying the same adventures I was, she laughed and congratulated me over the phone. She said things were looking up and she and her husband were back in the saddle.

There are very few people I can talk to—I mean, really talk to—about sex: my sister and this friend. That's about it. Like most young girls, I probably got most of my sex education from playground chatter and comparing notes with other girls. But sex is still a taboo subject among adults; it is no wonder we have difficulty discussing it with our daughters or in the health classroom.

If you read women's magazines, it seems as if all women are always ready all the time. The reality is much different. Issues of anger over household chores, childcare, laundry, workaholism, and overcrowded schedules have more to do with the frequency of sex in most households than anything else. It took me a long time to realize that one of the reasons I didn't want sex in those baby years was because I resented my husband for not doing as much work as I did to raise the children. And much of that anger was exacerbated because I was tired from getting out of bed in the middle of the night to nurse the baby.

I value having a friend who can discuss sex with me. We can still blush, use euphemisms, and skip the intimate details that might embarrass us, but we can also talk about what is behind our anger, our newfound passion, or our dead libido. We can help each other have a better marriage. We can grow and heal together. But we have an unusual friendship that has a very high level of trust. Only a few sisters, biological or otherwise, can share that.

We take each other through the peaks and valleys of life, sometimes as tour guide and sometimes as audience. What a great gift of a friend. And my husband thanks her too.

• • •

Making the Bed: Points to Ponder

1. Sometimes two people in a committed relationship find that their sex life is affected when the balance of power in the relationship shifts. Agree or disagree with this statement and provide specific examples.

2. Do you find sex a joy? What things put you in or out of the mood?

3. Do you have a friend, other than your partner, with whom you can discuss your sex life?

4. At what times are you "too tired," have a headache, or are not interested in sex because of your mood?

5. What things are you likely to do or talk about with your spouse after sex? Is there a different level of intimacy after sex?

6. Read the Song of Solomon. What is God's perspective on sex?

Welcome to the Club

"Jerusalem, Jerusalem, the city that kills the prophets and
stones those who are sent to it! How often have I desired to gather
your children together as a hen gathers her brood under her wings,
and you were not willing!"

—*Matthew 23:37*

WHEN I WAS A CHILD, I WANTED TO BE A MOTHER SOMEDAY.
When I was in my twenties, mothering looked like too much
work. When my sister lost a baby, then had a premature baby
with severe colic and some health challenges, I knew that I'd
better be pretty serious about it if I decided to have children. I
thought I'd make a much better aunt. But a charming, father-
able husband and my biological clock conspired together to
bring the three greatest gifts I have ever received, my kids.

I enjoyed my pregnancies and overindulged in food so that I
gained fifty-three pounds, forty-three pounds, and forty pounds
respectively. At least I tapered off some in my eating after learning how hard it is to take off that postbaby fat. "Eating for two"
was my mantra, and I knew I needed two pieces of chicken, two
helpings of mashed potatoes, and two pieces of cheesecake to
feed the inner child—not to mention the baby.

During my third pregnancy, I alternately endured and
enjoyed five weeks of bed rest at my doctor's bequest. I didn't

realize how tired I was from working full-time, caring for two preschool boys, and lugging around all that extra weight. I watched more daytime TV than a person should have to stomach and went back to work a week before I had the baby.

Having my first child was life changing. My first few moments as a mother were surreal. After I labored for twenty-seven hours and heaved and pushed for three hours more, the doctors prepared the delivery room for a Caesarean section. Three minutes before they had planned to slice me open, I threw up and in the course of it pushed more effectively. (It's not like doing a sit-up; it's like having a bowel movement. Why didn't someone tell me that three hours before?!) I had a healthy, eight pound eight ounce baby boy. They put this red, slimy, moving thing on my chest, and I wasn't quite sure what to do. I didn't have love at first sight; I was still in shock. Plus, my body hurt. I gave him a cursory glance, thought "Oh," and gave him back to the nurse. After delivering the placenta and being stitched up, I was more prepared to see this baby but still felt like an actor playing the part of a mother more than I was a mother myself.

My sister called me that night, and the first thing she said was, "Welcome to the club." I didn't know there was a club and was not sure yet what the membership dues were, but I thanked her all the same.

As my children have grown, I have done, in turns, a fabulous job and an embarrassingly lousy job in my parenting. There never seems to be a right answer to the constant stream of challenges and questions that face me as a mother: to let them cry or to pick them up, to let them sleep in my bed or face their monsters alone, to blow off the dirt or let them eat the ice cream that fell on the floor. My attitudes have changed and relaxed with each successive child, and I still hear myself using the phrases my own mother used on me: "If I were you, young lady, . . ." when she was mad, "Another day in which to excel" when I was going off to school, and "Be ever so . . ." when I was walking out the door. It was as if she wanted me to finish that last sentence for her and think to myself "careful" and then be careful because I had thought of it myself. Clever, that.

As a seasoned mother now, I can only vaguely remember what it was like to be able to go out without consulting a sitter, to have a car that was clean, to do fewer than ten loads of laundry a week, or to walk, not run, through the candy aisle. My children are still very young—nine, seven, and four. But when my husband and I had to switch from a man-to-man defense with our two boys to a zone defense with the addition of a third child, I got more efficient and more realistic in my parental expectations.

I am just a bit embarrassed to admit that I was pining for a baby girl after having two boys. I love my boys and who they are. I love the mother I am to them. But I am different with my little girl, and she brings out things in me that remind me of my own carefree girlhood. She giggles about her hair (boys just use spit and call it good). She sits up in her bed at night and talks about her day to her stuffed animals (the boys did this too, but they would change the ending to include a rocket blasting off or a car crash). When I am quiet, she asks me often if I am mad. She asks me to smile if I haven't in a while, and she loves lipstick, particularly all the way down to her chin.

My boys bring me daisies and caress my hair. My girl keeps the flowers for herself and asks me to put them in her hair. My boys wrestle with their dad. My girl does too but shrieks more and at a higher pitch. My girl loves to wear her church dresses, and my boys love to tell her how beautiful she looks—while they are content to wear holey jeans and a Nintendo or Jar-Jar Binks T-shirt to church. When my second son was three, he wore a Superman costume every day for a year. We owned several versions: long and short sleeved, long pants and shorts, cape and no cape. I wasn't sure whether I should be proud of his imagination or embarrassed that everyone thought he only had one change of clothing.

We are now officially in the "golden years" of raising children—between diapers and dating. Things are relatively easy, tempers are quickly appeased, and battles are over after a few visits from the tickle monster. We are done with the exhausting, sleep-deprived infant years and have not yet worried about who is making out in the driveway. Sure, the playground taunting or the complaints from too much homework are true "felt pain," but it feels good, in an "I know more than you" way, to tell them that things could be a lot worse for them.

My biggest concern for my children (other than the what-used-to-be-irrational "someone will shoot them at school or abduct them from the playground" thoughts) is that they have too much "stuff," spend too much time in front of the TV, Nintendo, or computer, and don't have the time or safety to build relationships with older adults and other families. Those privileges that I had seem to be lost. There are no block baseball games, no pickup basketball or bike-riding adventures. Their playtime is rigidly structured and supervised. They are not care-free, nor does their schedule allow them the freedom to explore their natural world.

Worrying is one of the privileges of being a member of the club. Parents get to worry about monsters that are real and monsters that are imagined—but don't ever figure out the difference until something really scary happens.

Every night before my children go to sleep, we pray togeth-er—sometimes all five of us together, sometimes just Mom or Dad with each child. Our prayers always start the same way: "Lord Jesus, thank you for this nice day. Thank you for Nathaniel, thank you for Mommy, thank you for Timothy, thank you for Daddy, thank you for Diana, thank you for Mor-timer [our dog]." We alternate giving thanks by name, the par-ents for the children and the children for the parents and the dog. We then pray for any combination of relatives and friends, always ending with a request for "a nice rest, good dreams, and keep us safe. In Jesus' name. Amen."

Instilling a sense of gratitude in my children is one of the most important things I try to do as a mother. I am so deeply grateful for the gift of my children and the change they have made in my life. They have brought me joys I could have nev-er imagined and frustrations I cannot describe.

If I can, as their mother, show my children the power of Jesus to shape their lives, to give them hope, and to walk with them through the valley of the shadow of death, I will have unparal-leled success as a mother. And that is my own little prayer as I lay me down to sleep.

• • •

Being a "B" Person

Joy and sadness come by turns, I know now. Beauty and bravery make you sad, Sharon's beauty and my aunt's bravery, and victory breaks your heart.
—*Walker Percy,* The Moviegoer

YESTERDAY MARYBETH CAME HOME FROM SCHOOL, TOLD ME that she had walked up to a group of girls, and said hi. One of the girls turned to her and said, "This is an A conversation, and you are a B person." I asked my daughter, stomach churning, what she had replied. "Nothing," she shrugged, "What could I say?" So I asked her if she was okay, if she had hurt feelings. "No," she said, "Whatever."

I guess I'm not sure what it means to be a preteen anymore. My daughter knows how to field mean-spirited comments without breaking stride. She dresses every day, picks up her backpack, and waits patiently for the bus. I feel like she is going to a war zone. I want to raise up an imaginary wand and place a protective armor around her. I want the "A" people to miraculously transform. If she read this, my daughter would sigh and say, "Oh, Mom, I'm fine. Really."

Marybeth tells me that she likes her life and her friends and, most of the time, herself. I, in the meantime, watch for cracks in her surface. I examine her as I imagine archaeologists study fossils, carefully and in detail, to make sure that today's fissures are not too deep, that the daily surface wounds are healing.

I have seen so many damaged girls and women. I have had girls in class who were afraid to raise their hands. When I call on them, gently, their voices shake when they answer. They are so afraid of ridicule, or of being wrong. I have had girls in my classes who pretended not to care, covering depression with hostility toward me, toward the class. In my office, they often swallow rapidly and try not to cry. In the reading journals that I often ask adult students to keep, women tell me regularly of regret, loss, that if they could do it over again, they would not get married or would have married someone else, would have pursued a career for themselves, would have taken better care of themselves, but now it's too late. The kids are teens, the marriage is stale, and wrinkles are facts. I tell them, in the margins, that there is plenty of time left. They mostly don't believe me.

A few lucky ones walk with confidence, smile with joy, and anticipate the future. But they are so few, and I watch my daughters try to grapple with a world that will by and large tell them that their greatest power is sexual and that growing older is a sin. The world will tell them that if they marry, they should assume their husband's names and to some extent his identity, and if they don't marry, they are undesirable. They will enter a world where, if they have children, they will be told they are without economic value if they stay home with the children and are not placing enough value on their children if they work. They will be told to keep their bodies and their chins firm and to, above all, never be angry. Angry women are one of our society's greatest fears.

"Take Our Daughters to Work Day" is coming up soon. My sister asked me the other day why feminists were excluding boys. "It's not fair, Jane," she said to me, "How do you think it makes the boys feel when all the girls are gone for the day?" I feel the immediate surge of anger, followed by the accompanying weariness, so that I can no longer distinguish the feelings of anger from the weary (so this is middle age). I try to explain, without showing any anger, that from the ages of nine to fifteen, girls' self-esteem plummets. Boys' self-esteem, on the other hand, increases. This isn't fair either. "Take Our Daughters to Work Day" is an attempt to counter society's messages to girls about their access to the world. It is not about hating men or boys, as I often reiterate to classes; it is about caring for women. Because our society doesn't do much of it, we have to fill in the gaps.

I used to believe that if I read the right books and parented in the right ways and participated in "Take Our Daughters to Work Day," my children would be invincible. Like most new mothers, I refused to believe my sisters when they told me that my children were born with inherent characteristics. I ignored their advice as their older children did things that I knew without a doubt my children would never do because I wasn't going to allow them to watch Disney or play with gender-specific toys. They laughed (not even gently), and I remained firm for all of about two years. At the age of about two and a half, Marybeth pulled a bedraggled baby doll from my sister's children's toy box and, holding it tightly to her chest, said, "Me baby." She cried when I tried to take it away from her, and so I began the first of many capitulations when my theoretical parenting confronted my children's realities.

By the time my second daughter, Erin, was born, we owned almost every Disney movie and had reams of baby dolls, clothes, and other plastic baby toy paraphernalia. I remember smiling when I read about a mother who had forbidden her boys to play with guns. Her four-year-old son picked up a fork at dinnertime, pointed it at his little brother, and said, "After dinner we're playing cops and robbers. This is my gun."

I wanted to mold my children the way that I have always accused men of attempting to create the women they marry. I should have known better. I deconstructed *My Fair Lady* in exquisite detail, but I never made the connection between men's attempts to create the "perfect wife" and my own desires to create perfect children. I believed that I could, by sheer willpower and proper training, turn out articulate, attractive, and intelligent children. Experienced parents are already grinning.

What I have inside my cluttered and often unvacuumed home are two articulate, attractive, and intelligent children. They just don't always demonstrate these traits in the ways that I originally envisioned them.

Recently I listened to a local child psychologist lecture one of our graduate classes about discipline. This man believes that about 80 percent of a child's personality and/or development is genetic; in other words, there's about 20 percent to play with. Twenty percent isn't much. So I do attempt to let my children create their own selves, although they would most likely disagree. Basic manners and the notion that they are not the center of the universe are about the only ideas I still attempt to hammer into my girls.

But I do worry about the world hammering at them. When other children say hurtful things, like "You're a B person," I fear that I have not adequately prepared my children to fight back. I grew up in a time and place where people might whisper things behind your back, but they rarely said anything to your face. I don't know what the proper response is or should be to that comment. However, if I've said anything to my girls more than a thousand times, it's "Be your own person."

So why should I be concerned when other people notice that they are?

• • •

Parenting 101: Points to Ponder

1. What parts of your personality do you believe to be influenced by nature vs. nurture, or genetics vs. the environment in which you were raised?
2. How has your self-esteem changed over the stages of your life?
3. Has your parenting experience been what you expected? Explain your response.
4. When have your children disappointed you?
5. At what age should a mother stop giving her children advice?
6. Read Genesis 16–17 and Genesis 22. Does this style of parenting in these stories clash with your own? If so, how?

Choosing Purple

There were places she still could not bear to be touched. Her belly, for one. Her belly stuck out too much, she was ashamed of it, could not accept the idea that it was anything but hideous.

—*Rebecca Wells*, The Divine Secrets of the Ya-Ya Sisterhood

I AM CURRENTLY AT SUCH A GREAT PLACE WITH MY BODY. I only moderately hate the cellulite on my thighs and butt; I have stopped wearing underwire bras, and my thinning hair poses only passing angst. It has not always been so.

Like most young girls, I loved my body until about the age of twelve or thirteen. I loved the way it moved, felt, and looked. The summer after sixth grade I began to hate the fact that I was hairy. I had to shave my legs and armpits at least once a day and fretted that hair on my upper lip was getting darker. Like many girls, the hate only intensified. Why couldn't I be thinner? Why couldn't my breasts be bigger? Why did my butt have to be so wide? Why couldn't my ankles be smaller? My desire to have my body look the girls in *Seventeen* was all-consuming. I dieted continuously and began that rocky road that most women travel. If I felt "thin," I was happy. If I felt "fat," I was miserable. My life revolved around what I could and could not eat.

Then I went to college and walked into my first of many classes in women's studies. I learned that my desire to look like a model was simply Madison Avenue's way of making money. Thousands and thousands of dollars are spent to make girls and women feel badly about themselves so that they will buy products in order to make corporations and stockholders wealthy. I became angry. I stopped shaving my legs and armpits. I stopped buying the "in" fashions and attempted to wear what I liked, what felt good on my body. I refused to buy any more *Glamour* or *Cosmo* or *Seventeen*. I found a wonderful book called *Diets Don't Work,* and I practiced eating only when I felt hungry and then eating whatever my stomach seemed to want. If it wanted ice cream at ten in the morning, then to the Dairy Barn I went. It took me about two years, but I finally let go of any and all attempts to diet. It was and still is one of the most freeing things I have ever done.

I did and still do a great deal of mirror work. Because we live in a society that constantly tells women that something is always wrong, at least once a day I look in the mirror and say, "You look great today, darling." Another book that helped me develop in this area has been *Learning to Love Yourself* by Louise Hay. I think that this book should be required reading for all teenage girls and that they should keep a copy of the book by their bedside table to counteract all the messages that are so hurtful to women.

When I teach gender studies courses, students usually respond to my lecture about the horrific messages women receive in our culture with "But don't men receive bad messages too?" The person who asks will almost always be female. And I respond, "Yes, there are hurtful messages to men, but not nearly to the extent, both in terms of volume and intent, that there are to women." I want to tell the student, and I hope that by the end of the course she will understand it herself, that the culture so implants in women the notion that they must care for men that she does not even understand that she is coming to the aid of men when she, herself, is so much more at risk. Women sit in class drinking Diet Coke after Diet Pepsi and ask me if men don't feel the same amount of pressure to be thin that women do. I generally then ask how many men drink diet sodas. Very few traditionally aged college men drink diet soda. I ask them why that is so. What we come to is, of course, that it is much more important for women to look good than it is for men. What we are talking about is power.

Men can be old, fat, bald, stooped, have hair growing out of their nose and ears, and still be considered successful. Women may not want to have sex with them, but society still regards them as successful as long as they have some amount of money and position. And trophy wives can usually be found. Women, on the other hand, are not supposed to age, go bald, get fat, or have hair in any unsightly places. One year not too long ago Sean Connery at the age of sixty-seven was voted the most sexy man in America. Egads, women!

At any rate, the more I understand that no matter how hard I try to look like the stereotypical model of beauty I will fail, the less I try. This has been a long adventure, but most definitely a worthwhile one.

My oldest daughter said to me recently, "Mom, that outfit you have on is kind of in style." I looked down at my jeans, purchased on sale, and a white hand-me-down shirt. "I am? What do you know," I laughed. Though she denies it at times, she is

glad that I do not buy into the beauty and fashion game. I do try
to buy my clothes on sale, and I don't buy expensive brands, but
I attempt to look average. I don't want to humiliate my girls, but
I do want them to know that I make up my own mind about
clothes, fashion, beauty—that I set my own standards. I tell my
children that I love being thirty-three, that the wrinkles at the
corners of my eyes are from smiling, and that I would not be me
without them. I want my daughters to look forward to growing
old, and if they are to do that, then they must see me enjoying
being in my thirties, forties, and so on. They need to see me
laugh and enjoy my body as it gets heavier, droopier, and more
relaxed. In our society men typically gain in power and prestige
as they age, and women typically lose power with every year.

I don't care what society says (or at least I am surely on my
journey away from it), and as the grand woman wrote in her
famous poem, I intend to wear a lot of purple.

• • •

Some Body

Or do you not know that your body is a temple of the Holy Spirit within
you, which you have from God, and that you are not your own?
—*1 Corinthians 6:19*

I HAVE BEEN TAUGHT WELL THAT WE ARE MADE IN THE *IMAGO DEI*,
the image of God. "Male and female God created them" says
the verse. And yet, if I were made in the image of God, could
my proportions be imperfect? I think a perfect God would have
created a better waistline than mine.

Let's face it. The bombardment of media images does not tout *imago Dei;* the images sell *imago Sex.* Because I am a product of both a beneficent Creator and TV and magazine pop culture, I am both proud of my body and disgusted by it at the same time. How can this be? How can I question that God knew what God was doing when my DNA was knit together in my mother's womb (Jeremiah 1:5)? I can, and do. Is that a sin?

My concerns are petty. I don't suffer from cerebral palsy, spina bifida, or congenital anything. On some days, I even think I'm moderately attractive, especially when I can suck my stomach in and am wearing a padded bra. Those are the best days.

I work out, eat well, and care about how I look. Sometimes.

I have been in two different careers that were dominated by men—first as an engineer and then as a pastor. I started to define myself by the male agenda. I never became gender confused, but I was heavily influenced by the prevailing definitions of success, beauty, and wealth. And I bought into it.

My great awakening came when I was pregnant with my first child. My stomach protruded way beyond my bustline, and that was how it was supposed to be. I realized that this is, in part, what a woman is: an incubator. I looked the part, and I was proud of my belly and even the way I waddled. I am not sure if it was hormones, sleep deprivation, or circumstance that transformed me into a mother, but I made the leap to self-awareness that my body shape really wasn't that important. It was true that you didn't have to have a DD cup to nurse a baby. Mine were small, but mighty, and produced life-giving milk.

It is easy to say body image doesn't matter when you are beyond the point of trying to look attractive for the rest of the world. I've been fat, and I've been thin. I prefer thin—mostly because it is easier to get around and my thighs don't rub together as much. I feel better too.

I do marvel at the miracle of life. I marvel at the way we have sabotaged women's ideas of the perfect body. We have taken a great and wonderful thing, the human body, and objectified it so we can sell more cars and other commodities.

I think I am beginning to understand part of what it means to be created in the image of God. We are creative, sentient, spiritual beings. The trick is to separate the images that titillate us from the image in which we were made.

No small task.

• • •

Mirror, Mirror: Points to Ponder

1. Our culture surrounds us with images of stereotypically "beautiful" women. These women are often a plastic surgeon's creation, and yet these are the only images we see. How can women re-create a realistic "beautiful" body image for our children and ourselves?

2. Whenever I walk by a mirror, I say to my image, "You look great today," or something funny and positive. This reminds me not to judge myself by the media's standards and usually makes me smile. It is important for us to learn how to reaffirm ourselves. Ponder some ways to accomplish this affirmation for yourself and important women in your life.

3. How would you describe your body?

4. How has your body changed over your lifetime?

5. What defines "beauty"? How are you influenced by media?

6. Read Song of Solomon 7:1-8 and 1 Samuel 16:1-13. How do you think God perceives our beauty?

Casserole Brigade

Now during those days, when the disciples were increasing in number, the Hellenists complained against the Hebrews because their widows were being neglected in the daily distribution of food. And the twelve called together the whole community of the disciples and said, "It is not right that we should neglect the word of God in order to wait on tables. Therefore, friends, select from among yourselves seven men of good standing, full of the Spirit and of wisdom, whom we may appoint to this task, while we, for our part, will devote ourselves to prayer and to serving the word."

—Acts 6:1-4

I LOVED IT. WOMEN BRINGING FOOD OVER EVERY NIGHT, disposable pans, dishes I'd never dream of cooking, desserts I shouldn't eat but did. When I was on bed rest for five weeks while pregnant, my church took grand care of me. That was the most recent time I enjoyed it.

The first time I was the recipient of the casserole brigade was when I was a new mother. The church we served at that time set the tone for what to expect when one was ill. I had never been a part of this form of caring before. Hot plates, butternut squash, several forms of pasta, and brownies that soothed the savage hormones—what a blessing. We quickly learned, however, that you can't get food from an entire church for several nights in a row. If you didn't eat the pork chops and zucchini from the Andersons on Monday night or by Tuesday lunch, you had to throw it out or freeze the leftovers because the Mitchells were bringing tortellini and green beans in a few hours and would need the counter space, if nothing else. Every other night is ideal for crisis meals on wheels. I remember my freezer being so full of stockpiled breast milk for the baby and lasagna for my family that we simply had no room for ice cubes.

We received numerous gifts of blankets, diapers, and mobiles. But the ones I appreciated the most were the ones that took the human touch. Of course, the casserole brigade was high on the list. But even better was an offer to baby-sit for a few hours. And best of all, the number one gift of all time in my book was one parishioner's offer to pay someone to clean my house while I was on bed rest. That parishioner got it. She understood what it meant to care for me in my time of need. I still remember her act of kindness. I think I'll write her another thank-you note.

No one in my family has ever been desperately ill, fortunately. We've had our share of colds and flu but nothing that even comes close to the kind of suffering I see when I visit my friends and church members in hospitals and nursing homes. I see all the things the doctor sees: Alzheimer's, Parkinson's, cancer, heart attacks, accident victims, and stillborn babies. And I see how the whole family is affected, not just the patient. I hear the conversations in the hallway and the whispers of the nurses. I see at-home preparations for the dying child. I see the empty chair on holidays and in the church pew. I see the former-mistress-now-second-wife. I see the limps, the canes, and the wheelchairs. I see the decrease in mental faculties and the bills for the nursing home. I see the wills and the cemetery plots. I see sadness and suffering.

And through it all, I see food. People bring plates and bowls of food. Tables groan with the weight of it; refrigerators and freezers bulge with the surplus. Cookies go stale, and Jell-o really does mold. A fifth of scotch seems to go pretty fast, as does a six-pack. But other than that, there is only so much food you can consume to make yourself feel better when life gets ugly.

In a time when there seems to be a lot of "chicken soup for the soul," people use food as spiritual and emotional comfort. Plus, it gives you something to say other than "I'm so sorry." Instead, you can say, "I know you are having a tough time, so I added a little bit of extra dry mustard in my deviled eggs that I know you like so well. Let me know if there is anything else I can do."

Usually, there isn't much you can do in the face of suffering. There are typically no "right" words to say or ways to care. But bringing food seems to be the gesture we offer that makes everyone happy. There is joy in cooking; there is comfort in receiving. Preparing a meal for others, who happen to be so preoccupied with their own crisis that they would probably be eating vending machine Doritos and powdered coffee for dinner if it weren't for you, makes you feel good about yourself. And the recipients, if they don't care for liver and onions, beet salad, and the Brussels sprouts that you brought, can use the menu to laugh about when things get really bleak. (Remember the tuna casserole Mrs. Bowers brought? She forgot to boil the pasta first and just covered the brittle baked pieces with extra cheese? I thought I'd never stop laughing. Good thing she can't see too well.)

We long to care for the ones we love but sometimes can't figure out what to do. A cake, a plate of ham sandwiches, or a gallon of milk can be a good excuse to show you care. And life has gotten even easier with the introduction of various disposable plastic containers. The recipient now doesn't have to worry about pans and lids getting back to their own home.

Prayers go to God, flowers and cards go to the heart, but food goes to the tummy. And knowing someone cares enough to bring their love in a casserole dish soothes the spirit.

• • •

Pampering the Guilt

"Quincy, time will teach you
that a woman's life is all about boundaries."
—*Wendy Wasserstein,* An American Daughter

SOMETIMES WOMEN'S WAYS OF CARING MAKE ME SCREAM. FOR example, take the assistant dean's birthday last Friday. We like her, and so we wanted to do something nice for her. The secretaries decided that they are going to bring in an Italian meal for lunch. Which means that I have to bring something. Which means that I have to get my kids off to school and then cook up a whole pile of fettuccine, which I was assigned to bring, and then go sit in a hallway and eat in nice clothes from a paper plate in my lap. The secretaries assigned the only male member of our staff, mind you, to bring apple cider. Why, oh why, couldn't we have just taken her out for lunch and all pitched in to pay for her meal? Drives me crazy.

Then there was the Pampered Chef party last Wednesday. Pampered Chef stuff is like Tupperware, only more expensive. Pampered Chef stuff is like Wal-Mart stuff, only more expensive. Pampered Chef–type parties are almost totally about guilt. Someone has a party because someone else begs her to, and she has it out of guilt. At any age, no woman truly needs a new cutting board that costs $29.95. You can get one at Target for about six bucks. No, the Pampered Chef host is begged by the Pampered Chef consultant to have a party, and the host feels guilty for saying no, which does not mean that she really said yes, but there you have it. Then the host sends out invitations to all her friends. Said friends get said invitation and groan. Said friends hope desperately that they have any excuse for not going. Said friends frantically try to remember whether the host came to the last Tupperware/baby shower/going-away party that they gave. Said friends say that, yes, they will come.

Meanwhile, the host has to prepare. The host must clean house, especially the kitchen, because fifteen to twenty women will have nothing better to do for the better part of two hours than inspect the host's kitchen for order, cleanliness, and refrigerator magnets. As soon as said friends respond to the invitation, the host starts to feel guilty. The host is basically inviting people to her house to lure them to spend money on things they don't need because she could not say no. The host buys lots of food, wine, and beer to account for said guilt.

Party time! Women arrive, hold a glass of wine (few drink it because most are on either Weight Watchers or the protein diet), and nibble on Dean and Deluca cheese and crackers. Then the party consultant (PC) starts demonstrating the products. She asks each woman to describe her favorite Pampered Chef item. Women flip frantically through the catalog attempting to locate something they own and have used at least once. "The stone," one woman cries out triumphantly, "I have the pizza stone." The PC is pleased. "And don't you just love it?" she crows. "Well," the woman looks down, "I kind of forgot that I had it. But the few times I did use it I really liked it." None of us wants to admit that we order pizza in and throw away the box. We don't need a pizza stone. "You can also bake cookies on it," the PC smiles at us. We nod obediently. The grocery store makes my cookies unless my twelve-year-old is in the mood, and I would not trust her with a stone that maintains heat temperature for hours and weighs more than my dachshund.

The PC continues. She talks about the egg slicer, the pizza roller (makes rolling on the stone easier), the oil spritzer (no more Pam), and the new items, like the Pampered Chef cookbooks, which show exclusively how to cook with Pampered Chef items. Eyes glaze. Breathing slows. The PC finally winds down and then tells us we can pay by check or MasterCard. We look at our order forms. We consider the amount of money the host spent at the last baby shower/Tupperware/engagement party we gave. We weigh how much we owe and look one last time through the now well-thumbed catalog to see if there is anything we could possibly buy as gifts. (Here, Thea, enjoy your new set of measuring cups. Merry Christmas.) We pick; we pay. We escape into the darkness of the evening and rest our heads momentarily on the steering wheel of our cars. We vow to never,

ever give another such party so that we don't ever, ever have to go to another one.

But it is only a momentary hope. We know that there will soon be another woman whose husband leaves her and who is frantically attempting to sell Pampered Chef products or candles so that she can stay home at least part-time with her children. We know that there will be a woman who is recovering from a nervous breakdown and needs to get some confidence back. We will go because our friend has a lump in her breast, a jerk for a husband, or a child who was recently arrested. We go because we care.

Sometimes our methods of caring, though, make me scream.

• • •

When You Care Enough to Spend the Very Most: Points to Ponder

1. What are a few events that you recall when people cared for you in extraordinary ways?

2. In what ways have you cared for others over the years?

3. How do men's and women's ways of caring differ? What accounts for the differences?

4. When do you participate in women's or men's gatherings that make you uncomfortable?

5. Have women's ways of caring changed as more women have entered the workforce?

6. Read Ruth 1. What commitment did Ruth have for her mother-in-law? Why did she have it?

Dead Psychiatrist in the Middle of the Road

"I'm thirty," I said.
"I'm five years too old to lie to myself and call it honor."
—*F. Scott Fitzgerald,* The Great Gatsby

SO THE OTHER DAY MY SISTER'S PSYCHIATRIST COMMITS suicide. She didn't know how he died. She happened to see his death in the obituary section and called me.

"He wasn't even sick," she said. "Did he have AIDS?"

I told her that I had no idea but that often people in such fields did have a higher rate of suicide.

"Oh, no," she told me, "he really had an understanding of life and people and how to handle things."

So I shut up, but I still had my suspicions. She called after the funeral. "He committed suicide." She felt betrayed, angry, sad. "How could he help me so much and not know how to help himself?" she asked. "How can I ever trust another therapist?"

I told her that many good therapists were left out there, minus one. She didn't find it funny, and I probably shouldn't have been so glib, but I have a stake in the "caring" professions as well. It's such a double bind for those of us who guide and "teach," whether it is mental health, academic learning, or spiritual guidance. On one hand, there is the undeniably ego-building effect of people looking up to me. They ask for my advice; they listen. They nod. They don't always do what I tell them, but they consider it. On the other hand, students often expect me to be "better," and they don't see me as a regular person who goes to the grocery store to buy green beans on sale, four cans for a dollar.

When I was in graduate school, I idolized a woman professor who taught postmodern literature. In the classroom she was smart, witty, funny, so . . . together. I wanted to be like her. I imagined her at home bantering ideas back and forth with her equally interesting husband and eating eclectic dishes for dinner. I imagined them in a contemporary loft with all glass and brass furniture and modernist paintings. When she invited our seminar group to her home for our last night of class, I couldn't wait. Now I would know how to decorate my house, what sorts of foods to buy for the pantry.

I pulled up in front of her house at dusk and was certain that I had the wrong place. The twenty-year-old split-level was painted a faded green, and the yard was tangled and needed mowing. The driveway was cracked, and the wrought iron stair railing was loose. I was confused. My discombobulating only continued as I entered the house. The carpet was old, the bathroom was pink, and the entire house smelled faintly of must. It was clean, but it looked like, well, God forbid, my parents' house, minus the yard and railing and cracked driveway (my parents were scrupulous about upkeep, if not decor). The professor was not nearly as witty at her home; she asked mundane questions about drinks and produced Cokes and Diet Cokes. The only thing about her house and the evening that even remotely suggested that she was the same person I thought I knew was the number of books in every room. But the stacks and piles of books looked like, well, God forbid, my house.

And the food! She had stale chips and some type of salsa. There was no pâté, no wine glasses, no elegant mushrooms caps stuffed delicately with minced garlic and sautéed bread crumbs and expensive cheeses. And the pantry! She had Hamburger Helper on her shelves (I couldn't help peeking). My idol ate Hamburger Helper. I couldn't quite take it all in. I decided she wasn't the person I wanted to imitate, after all, and I started scrutinizing other professors. I noticed their worn shoes and their dented cars. I became annoyed with their genteel poverty. I was sure that at Harvard and Yale there were professors who fit my ideal. I refused to believe that I would ever become like my fallen idol.

Today, I often invite my seminar classes over to the house on the last day of class. Occasionally I serve wine, but more often I don't. I certainly don't make pâté, and if I serve chips, there is a good chance they might be stale—it depends on whether or not my kids remember to put the chip clip back on the bag. I watch my students examine my house. We have old carpet, quite a bit of old furniture, and when it rains, my house smells faintly of dog urine. I often see in their eyes the same look that my professor must have seen in mine. They feel that I have failed them. What's the point, I know they think, of knowing all of the stuff you know if you still live just like I do? I don't answer their unspoken question because they wouldn't understand, or perhaps believe me, if I did.

If I did answer that question, however, I would tell them that I do live just like they do. I worry about my kids and my marriage and my cracking driveway just like they do. In the classroom they see me performing my job; it's what I'm good at. And I do love literature. My love for books is displayed in every room of my house and stacked in piles beside chairs and end tables. But outside of the classroom I go to parent-teacher conferences and the gynecologist and Target for shampoo. I learned one of my most important life lessons from that postmodern professor: people can be skilled in certain areas, but we all have some variation of Hamburger Helper in our cupboards.

When I saw a therapist during the final months of finishing my dissertation, she was enormously helpful. I was having anxiety that I wouldn't finish, and nightmares were plaguing me. I had also become recently aware that my hair was noticeably thinning, and I feared that I was not going to be attractive to my husband, or myself for that matter. The therapist had beautiful hair, thick and wavy. As I spoke of finding too many strands of hair in the shower, sink, etc., she played continuously with her own hair. Subconsciously, I am sure, she listened to my concerns and hoped that this particular malady would not also happen to her. Although she was my therapist, she was also human. I was able to take her advice and exercises about working through anxiety and make it useful to me. I didn't negate her for her very human failings.

And so I told my sister that her psychiatrist's suicide did not in any way negate the advice and help that he gave her. His life was not about his suicide, though his death was immeasurably sad. She said that countless patients stood up at his funeral and said how much this man had meant to them, how much he had given them. One woman said that he had given her back her life and she wished that he had been able to ask for help and receive it as she had from him. It's hard, though, when a person knows his or her area of expertise and then fails in it. It might not feel so bad for me to fail at art design, but I would be devastated if I felt that I had lost my ability to read and interpret literature. Perhaps that is how my sister's psychiatrist felt. The one area that he had confidence in failed him. He failed himself.

But I wish that I, too, could have thanked him for the comfort he gave my sister. I wish also that he could have held on long enough to learn to live with his failure. For I, too, have failed to become the erudite, glass-and-brass professor that I thought I would become. I muddle through English 101 papers and occasionally spill coffee on them. My husband and I don't banter nearly as much as we mutter. But in my failing is a greater, and I think better, appreciation for humanity. Part of my desire to be like the postmodern professor had to do with wanting to be "above" others; now I more enjoy simply being "with" people. It's still nice every now and then to have an adoring student, usually female, say in awe, "You know so much," but I don't delude myself about my real identity: Hamburger Helper shows up regularly on my pantry shelf.

• • •

Bad Counsel

But [Moses] said, "O my LORD, please send someone else."
—*Exodus 4:13*

"I'M SURE IT WAS GOD'S WILL FOR HER TO BE IN HEAVEN JUST now. God has a plan." This was the first, most memorable faux pas I committed in my ministry career. A nineteen-year-old girl, who had been in my youth group since she was sixteen and was a candlelighter in my wedding, died in a fiery small plane crash. I was on the telephone to her bereaved mother mourning with her, trying to offer comfort, and failing miserably.

It was the first time I had been chewed out by someone I was trying to help. When I offered that maybe God wanted Susie dead, which certainly sounds ridiculous now, her mother lit into me: "God did not want her to die! That is the most ridiculous thing I have ever heard. How dare you say that to me. You think that makes me feel better? Why would you say such a horrible thing? God did not want her to die any more than I did. This is not God's plan; this is a tragedy that breaks my heart."

I was stunned. I was, after all, only trying to help. But saying that her daughter's death had any merit was not particularly helpful to her. Her raven-haired, athletic, youngest daughter was gone. She was a talented dancer, innocent and charming, and just beginning her college career. The summer before, she had served on a mission trip to the underprivileged and had given countless hours to her church, even as a teen. She was a devoted young Christian woman with great promise. And she burned to death.

Thinking about these things in the abstract is all fine and good. It might be useful to opine that God has this all worked out, is sovereign, and that "we know that all things work together for good for those who love God, who are called according to [God's] purpose" (Romans 8:28). But these are hard truths to accept when faced with the tragedy of an unexpected death.

When a ninety-eight-year-old Alzheimer's patient dies, the

death is usually seen as a good thing. Granted, the person will be missed, and his or her death will leave a hole, but the suffering is over. When a baby or a teen or a mother of three dies unexpectedly, somehow the death is more keenly felt, more tragic, and all the more reason to persuade the cynics that God doesn't exist. After all, why would God let that happen?

A parishioner of mine, while watching the funeral of Payne Stewart, the professional golfer, husband, and father who died in a plane crash, asked me, "Why did God let him die?" My answer to her was not my usual, but true nonetheless: "Payne Stewart died because humans invented airplanes, and components of airplanes, which failed and so hurtled a man from thousands of feet up in the air crashing to the ground when the plane was no longer aeronautically sound." My point was that God didn't necessarily orchestrate the death as much as it was a result of God's allowing humans to create their own destiny on earth.

Sometimes I don't have anything better to say to comfort someone than the average person might. Sometimes I bite my tongue and can think of plenty to say when the church, filled with saints, gets crabby about the ratio of chocolate chip to oatmeal cookies after church and demands to know, "Who's in charge of that anyway?"

The amount of time we spend bickering over the color of paint in the ladies' rest room or the benefits of styrofoam or plastic cups is disheartening. I can't ever spout any biblical examples that would apply to these types of scenarios that would quiet the still sniping voice.

I guess my impression of ministry before I entered it and the realities of it now that I have been in it a while are vastly different. I assumed that since I would be working in a church, I would encounter no petty bickering, no politics, but would find an atmosphere of unconditional love. Right? Wrong. I did know ahead of time that there would be no "unsearchable riches" for a salary, but some of these other things took me by surprise.

A fellow pastor quipped, "The pastor's job would be great if it weren't for the people." True. But it is also true that the church members had expectations, however flawed, that their pastor wouldn't swear when she sprained her ankle or that she would always have something comforting to say in any situation.

One thing that we pastors have learned is the value of presence. Being truly "incarnational"—present in body and spirit—is the key to good ministry. As we were taught in seminary, "They don't care how much you know until they know how much you care." That is certainly true.

Jesus' incarnation is the model for good ministry. He was here. God came here. God didn't stop at sending a memo (the Ten Commandments). God didn't stop at the phone call (the call of Elijah), and God didn't quit after an e-mail (I suppose Pentecost is as close as I can compare to that). God sent God's own self: God in the flesh, Jesus. That is the key to connecting with the human race, being one with them.

Just this morning, I asked a dear friend and member who is going through a divorce a well-meaning but poorly worded question, "So what's wrong with you today?" Fortunately, she and I have talked for hours about her life, faith, and disappointments. She gave me a "Did you forget all your sensitivity training?" look, to which I stammered an apology. And then we both laughed. She knows I care. She also knows I'm human. And so we talked about what was wrong with her that day anyway.

On-the-Job Training: Points to Ponder

1. How can you respond to a person who asks you why God allows a talented young girl to die and murderers to live past eighty?

2. When you were in need of comfort, who or what helped you through the grieving process? What are some ways that you can be helpful to others in times of loss?

3. What roles do you find yourself in right now (parent, spouse, employee, supervisor, church worker, volunteer, chauffeur, grocery shopper, etc.)?

4. What things are different about your roles than you thought they would be when you started?

5. What do you fantasize about in others' lives or careers that you think would be better than what you have?

6. Read Romans 12:1. How does this verse challenge your self-perception?

To My First Love

If we confess our sins, he who is faithful and just will forgive us our sins and cleanse us from all unrighteousness.

—1 John 1:9

I STILL HAVE REGRETS—NOT ABOUT HOW MY LIFE TURNED OUT without you, but that I caused you pain.

You were my first true love. I had practice kisses before and dates with upperclassmen, but you were the first one to whom I gave my heart. You were the first man with whom I shared my hopes, dreams, fears, and principles. We were very innocent, you and I. And you had already made the difficult bridge from boyhood to manhood, but I was just beginning on my own journey.

When I was seventeen, you were twenty-three. You had miraculously kept yourself pure through college—unscathed and unmarried. I was in high school. We had to keep our romance a secret because of the stigma of the difference in our ages at a very vulnerable time in a seventeen-year-old's life.

You and I were different. The depth of our love was greater than the span of our ages or the flood of our hormones. Our innocence was our strength.

I remember one of the first times I got to ride on the back of your motorcycle. I tentatively placed my hands around your waist and brushed against you. The euphoria was overwhelming.

Holding you close and feeling the freedom of the country road gave me a sense of joy I will never forget. It was before we had held hands, before we ever kissed, and before I knew I would come to love you.

I remember meeting clandestinely in the city cemetery so we could have some quiet time together without causing gossip. Of course, someone else happened to come along, and you made conversation with them while I ducked behind a tombstone. That was a memorable event as well—especially when you left with them and I rode home alone on my bike half-giggling at the high adventure of it all and half-terrified of the dark.

I remember the trips to the lake with your family. I loved your little brother—and while you brought out the woman in me, when we all three played together, he brought out the child in both of us.

I marvel that you were so honorable. Both of us had declared that we did not want to have sex before marriage. But you were so handsome, so athletic. The temptation was strong. I am proud we did not falter. I am proud of you for your moral fiber. I am proud of myself for the times I kept my self-control.

But I am not proud of how it ended between us. We dated for four years. The two years I was in high school were easy. The two years I was in college were not. I was just beginning to understand all that the world had to offer. I wanted to explore, to find out what I thought of the world and what the world thought of me. I wanted to risk, to experience, to grow up. And yet I still wanted you.

You were so stable, so steady, so sure. I knew I could come back to you. So I used you as a tether to that which was safe and set out to discover whatever it was I was searching for. When it got too scary or too difficult, I would come home to loving arms. When I was feeling in control and independent, I would move further away from the love and safety I knew in you. I was not faithful. You were.

How can it be that you were so loving and so tender to me but that was not enough? Why did I feel the need to turn from my first true love?

You held me like a budding flower through my adolescence. You saw the blemishes on my face and my blossoming body in its awkward stages, and you called me beautiful. You were so much older and yet so innocent. You did not pluck me from the garden. Rather, I made you wither. I am so deeply sorry.

Twenty years have passed. I still carry the scars of tearing away from you. But I also carry the self-esteem, the confidence, and the knowledge that I shared a wonderful part of my life with so tender a person as you.

I am so different than when you knew me. I have explored, changed, studied, married, had three children, moved, traveled, grown, and made a lot more mistakes. But the very center of who I was, the one who shared your beliefs about fidelity and chastity, has come to be my center again. I swayed as a pendulum in finding out who I was. I took risks, made mistakes, made good and bad choices, and learned a lot along the way. But I now know that at seventeen I knew a lot more than I thought I did about what is good and right and how to behave.

I am so proud of you and your family. I chuckled when I learned you were marrying one of my high school friends. I wonder what it is about younger women that appeals to you.

Part of me wants to hope that you see some of me in her.

I am also proud of myself and my family. I have found a deeper love with my husband, a man more innocent than I. And maybe part of what I learned in our days together is the value of true love and the honor of commitment.

In the end, I found my heart's desire. My life is better for having known you. And I would not wish to take back our decision to break up. It is awkward to see you. I want you to know I am happy. I want to know you are too. But most of all, I want you to know how much I loved you. And how sorry I am that I hurt you.

• • •

To My Oldest Friend

Her old friend had come home. Sula. Who made her laugh, who made her see old things with new eyes, in whose presence she felt clever, gentle and a little raunchy. Sula, whose past she had lived through and with whom the present was a constant sharing of perceptions. Talking to Sula had always been a conversation with herself.

—*Toni Morrison, Sula*

WE MET IN THE THIRD GRADE. YOU HAD MUCH CUTER clothes than I did. I was jealous. Then you moved into my neighborhood. You had a prettier bedroom and parents who were fun, and I was still envious but tried to ignore it.

Then your parents divorced. You moved twice in two years, and your mother remarried. You spent the night at my house quite a bit. You wet the bed once, and I pretended not to notice.

We became better friends.

We went to middle school together. We talked about what to wear the first day of school, and we matched our tennis shoes to our corduroy pants. We still played with Barbies, but we didn't tell anyone. We loved board games and cards. You developed early, and I was jealous. You had the first boyfriend, and I felt left out. We never talked about it.

We went to high school, and by then I had developed. I started running around with a different group of girls—girls that drank beer and car dated. You were much more of a studious girl; you liked math and did well in it. I met Wayne, and we started dating exclusively. I know you felt left out. We never talked about it.

We went to college together and were freshman roomies in the dorm. We went through sorority rush, and I was rushed harder than you were. I pledged a house with a better reputation, but you became treasurer in yours.

We both excelled in college, but you were the business major. You landed a job with a then Big Eight accounting firm, and I went on to graduate school in English. While you were making strides in your career, I married Wayne, had one baby and then another, and kept working on my Ph.D. When I talked to you during this time, I felt like we were on different planets. My days were about potty training, getting Marybeth to quit sucking her thumb, and semiotic theory; you were accumulating money and nice furniture. You got married, and I was a bridesmaid. I was so happy for you—and excited that perhaps our friendship could come alive again.

You waited quite a while to have your son, but when he came

along, I was thrilled again—for you but also so that we could talk about raising children and marriage and the stuff that goes along with that. But you kept working full-time and doing so well at your job. Your son went to daycare full-time, and you didn't seem to have any of the guilt that I had when I put my kids in daycare. We didn't talk about it.

I finished my Ph.D. (finally!), and you came to the gradua-tion party. I didn't ever tell you about my doubts, my fears, and the nightmares that I would never finish or that I would fall apart during the defense. So you really didn't understand the relief and my utter joy that night.

And so, my oldest friend, I write to you to tell you that although I have known you for twenty-five years, I miss you. I don't feel comfortable enough to ask you whether you are plan-ning to have any more children. I don't feel close enough to you to ask you how your marriage is going. I don't know what makes you laugh anymore or how you handle juggling all that you do without going crazy.

There are walls between us, my friend, that I think have to do with competition and success and mothering and parenting. So can I be the one to say "uncle"? I don't care anymore who has the nicest house (you do) or the best-behaved children (depends on the age). I don't care who is aging faster or who has the best clothes. I don't want to compete with you anymore because I think that competition is part of what has happened to us all these years and what has finally driven us apart. We measured our success against each other. And while that propelled and compelled us to succeed, it also ruined any chances we had for real friendship.

I have spent the last year watching a dear friend battle breast cancer, and she is losing the fight. And as we approach our midthirties, I simply don't care much about what the world thinks of me. Or you. And maybe you don't feel the way I do. Perhaps you are just too busy to call me often, and when you do, you are too tired to talk about real things. Maybe you just don't want to be my friend anymore if I don't play the game we never talked about and perhaps only I thought we were playing.

But I say "uncle," and I hope we can now be "ollie, ollie, ollie, oxen free" like we were when we were kids. We have watched each other grow up, and I would like to do more than watch each other grow old. So please understand that if it is important to you, I hereby state that in the game of life you have won. You get to be all-time pitcher.

So how have you been?

Message in a Bottle: Points to Ponder

1. Who was your first love? What sorts of memories do you have of that time? What would you say to your first love if you could?

2. Often the media and advertising firms treat love and sex as if they were one and the same. Discuss the important differences between love and sex. Which one do you feel is most important?

3. What things have you done in your life that you still regret?

4. Have you sought forgiveness for those things?

5. Do you do things that you know you'll regret later? What tempts you? What things are the most difficult to turn away (food, sex, lottery tickets, a bargain sale, white lies, stealing, juicy gossip)?

6. Read 2 Corinthians 2:5-11. What does this passage bring to mind?

Nuremberg, Kansas

He flipped my shirt up over my head and jammed it into that hand.
I heard the sound of the belt swinging up, a song in the air, a high pitched
terrible sound. It hit me and I screamed. Daddy Glen swung his belt again.
I screamed at its passage through the air, screamed before it hit me.
I screamed for Mama. He was screaming with me, his great hoarse shouts
as loud as my high thin squeals, and behind us outside the locked door,
Reese was screaming too, and then Mama. All of us were screaming, and
no one could help.

—*Dorothy Allison*, Bastard out of Carolina

LAST WEEK WAYNE AND I WATCHED ALEC BALDWIN STAR IN
Nuremberg, or to be accurate to the German language, Nürnburg.
We do like to Americanize whenever possible. I was reminded of
a number of things when I watched the film, some of which, in
conversation, have provoked intense and irate discussion.

First, I was reminded of the time that I saw the 1961 film
Judgment at Nuremberg. I was thirteen years old, and it was
summertime. My older sister and I shared a room, and we had
a small black and white television set close to our bed. My sister read for a while and then went to sleep. I was watching a
rerun of something or other, and then *Judgment at Nuremberg*
came on. I watched the entire movie, fascinated, repelled, and
deeply moved. I had read *The Diary of Anne Frank* and other

novels that depicted the Holocaust, but nothing prepared me for that live footage of tractors shoveling dead bodies. I can't remember clearly whether it was the tone of the film or my own perception, but I felt that what I had witnessed was the incredible capacity of people's inhumanity to fellow humans, although I probably wouldn't have used those exact words. I didn't come away from that movie with an understanding that all Germans were evil, nor that all the Nazis were evil. Our capacity to inflict pain and our enjoyment of hurting others flickered quietly from the tiny television set, and I did not sleep much that night.

The Alec Baldwin film, in my opinion, was a feel-good film for Americans. At a time when racial conflict is still rippling across the nation without much thought of solutions, at a time when violence and school shootings have become commonplace, how nice to look back to a time when America appeared all good and the Nazis all evil. Nothing, but nothing, that happens here in America comes even close to resembling the dead bodies, the piles of gold teeth. Nothing comes close to the children gassed in death chambers, alone, crying for their mothers. Therefore, we can sigh and relax in our ultimate innocence, our saving graces, for after all, American soldiers did liberate the camps. Films like *Nuremberg* salve our collective consciousness. They reassure us of America's basic goodness, in spite of a problem here or there. The film reminds me of a thief who attempts to prove her innocence by pointing at a fellow criminal who stole more goods. We are not innocent here in America, but the publicity and the high ratings of shows like *Nuremberg* show us how desperately we want to be.

Toni Morrison, in her Pulitzer Prize–winning novel *Beloved*, draws parallel after parallel between the Holocaust in Germany and what she terms the American holocaust of enslaved black people. In a taped interview she asks her interviewer, and therefore those who watch the film, to imagine the Holocaust going on for three hundred years, as slavery did in this country. One of the opening pages of *Beloved* says simply "Sixty Million," and she is referring to one historian's estimate that sixty million African and African American people died as a result of slavery in America. The sixty million, of course, parallels the six million Jews who died in concentration camps, but Morrison continues throughout the book to document the "experiments" that were performed on slaves, the chains that many were forced to wear in "chain gangs" and other instruments of torture such as the "bit" that prohibited speech. I broached these parallels with a colleague who was enthusiastically recanting all the horrors of the Holocaust and the enjoyment with which he was watching the *Nuremberg* miniseries. After a significant pause, he said, "Well, you know, some people think that the number of abortions performed in the United States can also be compared to the Holocaust." Although I cannot comprehend how a woman's right to choose can be compared to slavery and concentration camps, I respectfully allowed him to attempt the comparison. However, more interesting to me was the immediate way in which he, and the others involved in the conversation, moved away from the subject of slavery and any implication that Americans were capable of cruelty in nearly the same vein as the Nazis.

Elie Wiesel and other Holocaust survivors want to keep the memory of the Holocaust alive so that the tragedy will never be repeated. I admire their attempts, and I agree with their philosophy. But as long as Americans, and any other non-German nations, watch the Holocaust films and go to the Holocaust Museum with the voyeuristic attitude that they are watching "evil" that was "over there," then I'm afraid we have all missed the point. The point is that within all of us exists the capacity for great cruelty. Some would call it sin. But whatever the terminology, it is not a specifically German trait.

I see the capacity for cruelty in my daughters' classrooms when they tell me of children taunting and teasing others in school and on the school bus. I occasionally see the flashes of cruelty in the way my children treat each other. I see adults build their own egos in meetings by making others look stupid or inadequate. My father used to tell us children when we were growing up that "absolute power corrupts absolutely." He memorized line upon line of poems and essays in the one-room schoolhouse he attended, and when he trotted out these bits of information, usually in the car on the way to a sporting event, we would roll our eyes. But, like many things parents say, the message lodged itself in some minute corner of my brain, and I wonder if Americans, guilty as sin for slavery, don't exalt ourselves in the cleansing waters of the Holocaust.

We watch the absolute power of Hitler, and we ignore the power that we have in our own society. We submerge ourselves in the cruelties of another people so that we can ignore the growing gap between the rich and the poor in our country. We watch children reach for their parents as they are marched into the gas chambers, and it doesn't seem to matter so much that many of us are not disciplining our own children or teaching them to be caring, considerate people.

I am not much of a Bible quoter, but there is a line somewhere that reads, "To whom much is given, much is also expected." Many of us in America who have been given much expect more to be given. The Nazis came to power and promised riches and respect to those who followed, with the exception of Jewish people. The Germans in power took what was being handed to them without thinking of the loss of others. As long as they were satisfied, many did not ask about the smoke coming from the other side of the fence topped with barbed wire. Do we not, as Americans, ignore our slums, our racial conflicts, and our children's increasing self-absorption as long as we have our comfortable salaries and increasingly lavish homes? We have been given much, those of us in middle- and upper-middle-class America. What do we willingly give back? When do we speak out for those who have little or no voice?

It seems to me, at age thirteen and today at thirty-three, that the lesson of the Holocaust is firstly about human beings' refusal to acknowledge other peoples' pain and loss and secondly about our refusal to take responsibility to alleviate that pain. We can bathe nightly in the atrocities of the Holocaust, but until we acknowledge the fact that the Holocaust could, and some people believe did, happen here, then we miss the entire message. We certainly cannot save the world, and I would never imply that all Americans need to sell their homes and give their money to the poor. However, sitting in our La-Z-Boy recliners while enjoying watching a film in which others commit atrocities points directly to our own collective disease. A black student said last night in class, "I think that racism is on the rise again. I think it is worse now than it was fifteen years ago." The only other black student nodded, the white students

103

shifted uneasily in their chairs, and then someone changed the subject. It is much easier to talk about the Holocaust and six million Jews who were annihilated in all kinds of revolting methods. We can talk about gas chambers and rifle squads while we eat lunch. Just don't mention racial discrimination. It might make us uncomfortable.

. . .

Unmasking Evil

Discipline yourselves, keep alert. Like a roaring lion your adversary the devil prowls around, looking for someone to devour.
—*1 Peter 5:8*

AT DIFFERENT TIMES IN MY LIFE, I HAVE FELT THAT I WAS TRULY in the presence of evil. What I experienced was not the scary feeling you get when watching a "scream" movie or when you are in the graveyard at night, but discernment that a dark force threatens your very soul.

The first time was when I was twenty-two years old. I was living large as a single career woman, traveling to new cities, learning about the world. I had an expense account and a whole world out there to explore. I realize now that I was much more naive than I thought I was.

I was flirting, literally, with evil. He was married with two children and was far too old for me. But he was rich, handsome, and paying an inordinate amount of attention to me. We had a grand time together. I flirted; he bought me things. What a great way to live. I was single, and if he was unhappy in his marriage, then that was his problem, and his wife's, not mine. Or so I thought.

One evening, we came precariously close to consummating this game we had been playing. We were sitting together on a couch in a very dark room. We were heady with excitement and pushing the boundaries of an "appropriate" relationship. It was electrifying. And we visited, danced, and drank the evening away. As we were inches apart, I looked into his eyes, and I knew what was coming next. Or at least I thought I did.

As I focused on his face, it turned evil. It was maniacal, contorted, and grotesque—not in real life, but in my imagination. It was as if I could see under the mask that was his face, and underneath it I saw death. It certainly didn't do much for the mood.

At first, I just thought my imagination was playing tricks on me. I tried to engage him again, but I realized that I was seeing into his soul. I had just begun to rekindle my Christian faith at that time in my life, and the temptation to bond with him certainly put a damper on that. I was a Christian. He was an avowed atheist. I was single; he was married. I was twenty-two; he was taking advantage of the fact that I was twenty-two.

I was so repulsed by this "vision" that I never saw him again—at least not in the way that I used to see him. He used to seem so glamorous, powerful, and attractive. Now he seemed to me like a bottomless pit of disease. I don't really know what happened that night, but I am grateful that I saw that situation for what it was. Wouldn't it have been a coup for the dark side to snatch me from my blossoming Christian faith and drag me into evil? I think more was at stake in that encounter than I could ever imagine.

It is much easier to define events, problems, or ideas as evil in hindsight than it is when you are in the middle of it. Looking back, of course, I see now that I was on the precipice of a chasm. I was flirting with my own balance, the gusts of wind, and feeling invincible. At the time, it just seemed like a lot of fun. I wouldn't have used the words "temptation," "sin," or "perversion." Heck, I just wanted to have a good time. It felt good, so I went for it.

I've gotten a lot of mileage out of that experience. It is a reminder to me that when we disregard what we know is good for us and fling ourselves headlong into what is not, we are flirting with much more than a potential sugar daddy.

People often bristle at the sexual boundaries that are written in the Bible. They are offended that anyone would dare to tell them what choices are "moral" and what choices are acceptable to the clan. They are independent and capable of making their own choices, good or bad. Ain't it the truth? We are capable of those choices. But without the distinctions between what is helpful or harmful spiritually, we get ourselves into situations far too deeply before we can extricate ourselves. And then we find ourselves praying for mercy.

I've always held that God's commandments, directions, and lessons are there for a reason. God knows what is good for us. Bedding another woman's husband isn't. It is that simple. I suppose many an affair has had a happy ending—but not for the one left behind. People recover, sure, but they are never the same.

I was taught boundaries as a child, and I tested them. I rebelled to the same degree most kids do. But I always knew what was right when I crossed over into what was wrong. I made some very bad choices, to be sure, and I still have the ugly memories to prove it.

I believe evil is present in more ways than we think. We white folks don't often see the evil of racism, even when we are standing right there in the customer service line behind the black man who can't make a return without a receipt even though the white woman in front of him could. We just assume there must have been some other reason. In some ways I wish I could see evil for what it is more often. But in other ways, it might be too frightening.

My response to evil in the world is twofold. First, I pray like mad that it might go away. When I am truly afraid, I say the name of Jesus. I know it has power that I'll never understand. I know that evil has been conquered by the resurrection of Christ. I take great encouragement from Martin Luther's hymn "A Mighty Fortress Is Our God." Its words are powerful, as is the name of Jesus:

> *Did we in our own strength confide,*
> > *Our striving would be losing;*
> *Were not the right man on our side,*
> > *The man of God's own choosing.*
> *Dost ask who that may be? Christ Jesus, it is He,*
> *Lord Sabaoth His name, From age to age the same,*
> *And He must win the battle.*
>
> *And though this world, with devils filled,*
> > *Should threaten to undo us,*
> *We will not fear, for God hath willed His truth*
> > *to triumph through us.*
> *The prince of darkness grim, We tremble not for him;*
> *His rage we can endure, For lo! his doom is sure:*
> *One little word shall fell him.*

"One little word shall fell him." It is the name of Jesus, and I say it if I need to. God is more powerful than any evil.

My second response to evil is to avoid it. But that means recognizing it first. Institutions do not have faces but can be evil or used for evil. How can I deal with that? Strangers who murder their children are plagued by evil thoughts and act on those. How can I respond to that? I can trust in the sovereignty of God and wait it out until Christ comes again. In the meantime, I don't flirt with other women's husbands, and I try to figure out why God doesn't want me to do all the other things that I think look like fun but have evil written all over their faces.

• • •

Devil with the Blue Dress: Points to Ponder

1. When have you judged others and failed to look within? What is the danger of seeing evil as "out there"?

2. Read Matthew 7:1-5. How have you failed to see your own faults?

3. The movie *Judgment at Nuremberg* describes the evil as it unfolded in Germany as "the absence of empathy." How would you define evil?

4. What would cause the German guards to imprison and torture Jews? What would cause the officers to command it or Hitler to design it?

5. When have your given in to peer pressure even when you disagreed with the group decision? Why did you give in?

6. At what times have you seen yourself become so immune to others' pain that you ignored it or even made it worse?

7. Read Philippians 2:1-11. Who is "every knee" and "every tongue"?

13 ├── A FACE IN THE CROWD

Loneliness

At my first defense no one came to my support,
but all deserted me. May it not be counted against them!
—*2 Timothy 4:16*

AFTER DRIVING BACK TO WORK FROM THE NURSING HOME, I
felt sad. Mrs. Jenkins was so lonely. Her husband had died nearly twenty years before, and her health was not great. She was still
sharp mentally and would ask me about old friends in the
church. She lamented about the death of her neighbor in the
next room on the third floor. But she was so lonely.

Mrs. Jenkins was a bit miffed that I hadn't visited her more
often, but then apologized and said, "I'm just a lonely old lady. I
know you are so busy." My emotions were mixed. I felt guilty that
I hadn't visited her more often, but she was relatively healthy,
hadn't been in the hospital recently, and had a few relatives who
visited her sporadically. But I know the weeks drag by at a glacial
pace when you are bored and miss the life you once had.

But part of me wanted Mrs. Jenkins to take more control of
her life. Every day she had access to scores of activities, book
clubs, bridge games, ice cream socials, and guest speakers. She
wouldn't go. She became increasingly isolated, and therefore
more lonely, with each passing month. She was physically able,
although perhaps occasionally incontinent. But every person in

the place struggled with the same issues. They all had some physical limitation, or they wouldn't be there.

Amazingly, being old wasn't the reason Mrs. Jenkins was lonely. It was her choice to be lonely. Granted, I'd have a hard time convincing her it was her choice. In fact, I never did. But she isn't the only lonely person out there. As I look at the lives of the people I care about, I sometimes get frustrated at the choices I see them making. No doubt, they could give me some good advice on my poor choices as well. But most of what bothers me is how little importance is placed on their own true, deeply human needs.

In the average suburb, residents place plenty of emphasis on how much money they make, how far they have to commute, or what color the carpeting should be to blend truly with the furniture ensemble. Advancing careers takes precedence over learning new things for the fun of it or keeping a good balance in every aspect of life.

I have a friend who spends all of her time from 3:30 to 9:00 P.M. shuttling her three children every day after school to and from play practice, dance, soccer, piano lessons, baseball, speech therapy, play group, and church. It doesn't seem that she or her children particularly thrive on these events, but she feels compelled to push them to try and experience all these things in order for her to be a good mother. She doesn't want her children to "miss out" or to get behind.

What bothers me most about overscheduled children and stressed-out parents is that one of the first casualties of busyness is friendships and community. If you invest forty-five minutes in soccer once or twice a week and then race to the next event, you aren't even enjoying the full benefit of being a part of a soccer team—that of being in and building a community of people who care about the same thing and about one another. I barely even know the other mothers on my son's soccer team because they are constantly flitting.

I think the overscheduled child is a symptom of the parents' need to fill their own lives with things and events, rather than people. People disappoint. People hurt your feelings. People make demands on your time. But people also can fill a deep need that each of us has for socialization.

Extended families are truncating; grandmothers, aunts, and cousins usually live in nursing homes or several states away, rather than in the next room, as might have been the case one hundred years ago. Church is no longer the heart of the community, as might once have been the case. People don't gather at block parties, at the neighbor's house, or around the pond like farmers and small-town citizens used to do.

Not only do we not share our lives with our neighbors across the street or across the hall; we don't even know their names. We have closed off our hearts, our emotions, and our interpersonal growth because we are too busy to make friends. We are too busy to invest our lives, give our time, and risk our emotions to build deep and lasting friendships with the people we see every day.

What could possibly have happened to make us shun one of the fundamental needs of human nature—to be in community? We have placed other things in priority over that ideal—perhaps because we cannot immediately see the inherent value in it or perhaps because we think we need to "do" instead of being content just to "be." Most of us should define ourselves as a human "doing," not a human "being."

We usually miss friendships the most during vacations, holidays, and snow days from work and school when we have hours of unstructured time on our hands. When we become empty nesters, we realize we have raised a family, built a business or career, but don't have anyone we could think of to call on a Saturday afternoon on the spur of the moment and invite to go shopping. We keep our divorces to ourselves, our child's medical problems under wraps, and our battle with alcoholism a secret because those things are too difficult to share. We don't have many people we can trust because we haven't invested the time in other people to even allow them to care about us.

I see many men and women live and die as lonely people. I see many people like Mrs. Jenkins who haven't learned, even when healthy, how to connect on a deep level with other human beings. Maybe part of the problem we have is we don't want people to see our warts or our Depends. We want to keep up the front, look good for others, and pretend we "have it all." We don't want people to see our humanness and our need for other people.

The great thing about Jesus' example to us is that he came and lived among us. He was a child. He certainly had needs, wet diapers, and a broken heart at times. And the power of Christ comes in his weakness. The very thing that makes him human and vulnerable makes him powerful. From his death came life. Have you ever noticed that you can bond quickly with someone who has shared a trip to the emergency room, a financial crisis, or other trauma? The strength of the bond is in the shared weakness. Our humanness makes us able to connect. And our need to connect makes us human.

• • •

In Bars There Is Truth

"You do not understand. This is a clean and pleasant café.
It is well lighted. The light is very good and also,
now there are shadows of the leaves."

—*Ernest Hemingway,* "A Clean, Well-Lighted Place"

I LOVE BARS, TAVERNS, LOUNGES, JOINTS, AND WHATEVER OTHER terminology people use to describe places where people gather to drink and converse. I love coffee shops too, but not nearly to the same extent. I know that bars are supposed to be dens of evil, but I have never really found that to be true. Instead, I find camaraderie in bars that I rarely experience anywhere else.

My love of taverns began in high school when my friends and I made fake IDs and drove over the Kansas bridge to Wathena, where the drinking age was eighteen and a bar called The Place did not look too long at our fake driver's licenses. Inside the bar we mostly certainly did drink beer, but, more importantly, we danced, played pool, and talked about life. I remember the last day of high school holding hands with my friends, boys and girls, and dancing to the "Hokey Pokey." The bar was a haven from watchful parents and weary teachers. Inside we were free to say what we wanted, to be who we wanted to be. Inside it did not matter who was going to college and who was not, who graduated fifteenth or fiftieth. The owners of the bar kept their eye on us, and during the two years that I went to the establishment, I never saw a fight, nor did anyone have an accident.

When I went to college, we often walked to a bar called the Fieldhouse, which was much more of a "meat market," or a

113

place where people went to find dates. Though I missed the homey atmosphere at The Place, there was undeniable excitement about dressing up and going to see if destiny was waiting behind a "dollar pitcher." Inside the bar were a DJ and scores of young people talking and posturing. It was also fun to "try on" different sorts of adult identities. Some nights I would pretend to be the dedicated student that I truly was, but other times I pretended to be a ditzy coed working on a Mrs. degree, which I assuredly was not. Again, though, the freedom to be silly or stupid or not myself offered relief from the pressures of academic study and the fear of failure. The Fieldhouse functioned as a place apart from regular society, and at times, I desperately needed that space.

A bar called the Heidelberg is where I went with Wayne to relax following a night of studying or to talk about whether or not we should marry. We dreamed many nights into the future over nachos and a beer. Our conversations were usually intense and often angst-filled as we wrestled with our differences in personalities, definitions of success, and how many children we eventually wanted. These talks simply would not have been the same in the institutional-smelling and -looking dorms. However, in a smoky, dark booth in the corner of the Heidelberg, I felt that the hours of the night were ours and we would find our way in them.

After we married and the babies were born, I relished our time in bars because there was generally not a crying baby in them. For about a five-year period, I never went to the bathroom, showered, or got dressed without someone in the room with me. I went to the bar to have a beer like a toddler to a puddle. Bars were where people talked about movies and careers. Fred P. Otts was my favorite bar during this time in my life. A small, neighborhood corner bar, P. Otts was rarely crowded. My sister and I would often go on a Friday night at happy hour and talk about our marriages, our extended family, and the cute shoes she saw on sale at the Jones Store. Our husbands would meet us after work, and if it was nice, we sat outside, pulled the weekend toward us, and wrapped it around our table like gossamer.

We go to the bar at the Doubletree now, more often than not. The P. Otts crowd seems a bit young and rowdy, and the music seems perhaps a bit too loud. We go to the hotel bar and sink down into the plush chairs and loveseats carefully arranged around coffee tables with silk arrangements on top. We drink more wine now than beer, and we occasionally even slip off our shoes and tuck our feet up under us as we sip a Chardonnay. Sometimes a pianist plays jazz in the background, and the music rolls around us and reminds us that life is wonderful, exotic, painful, and not, perchance, exactly the future we dreamed of in college. Then we talk about that.

Bars, lounges, taverns, joints, have long been places where I, and the people I meet there, are genuine. However, I know there is a darker, seedier side to bars, where people crave, not companionship, but alcohol. I know that bars are often where people meet to cheat on a spouse or to avoid dealing with issues in their lives. But give me a bar any day, with its infinite array of derivatives, rather than a PTA meeting, where parents compare clothes, cars, and college funds.

I also like to think, mostly at church, that Jesus would have frequented bars. Jesus liked to be where people were both laughing and hurting, where people were real, and bars contain much of both. I have this image of a woman, about to turn fifty, sitting on a barstool. I have seen her many times and in many places. She looks hard, has on too much makeup and too much Miss Clairol. She sits alone sipping a mixed drink and glances quickly each time the door opens to see if there is a possibility of a date. She has been married two or three times and has two or three grown children; none of it really worked out. I imagine a thirty-three-year-old man coming into the bar. He wears jeans and a baseball cap. He sits down beside her and orders a beer, perhaps a Miller. He grins at her and tells her that she is just the person he has been looking for. This woman is intrigued—no one has been looking just for her for a long time. She tells him that he must have the wrong person. She is weary, scared, and was not a very good mother. She smokes while she talks and gestures with her cigarette. She pauses and catches his eyes. They are staring at her intently, and he nods. "Yeah, some folks thought my mom wasn't so good either, but I tend to disagree." He offers to buy her dinner, and she says that from the look of him she had better pay. He replies, "Fine," and says he doesn't care one way or the other about money because there are too many more important things to consider. They go to a restaurant like Denny's and drink bottomless cups of coffee. She talks, he listens, and she cries. Gradually the makeup comes off on paper napkins, and she pushes her now disheveled hair behind her ears. Jesus holds her hand and tells her that the glass of water she raises to her lips is living water; it represents the beginning of a new life. The woman drinks the water, and they walk out into the night as the young man promises to stay in touch.

Funny, but I often feel closer to God in bars than in churches.

People at my church do well; they give donations to missions in Russia and create wonderful youth programs that our girls attend. We have beautiful tapestries and tons of parking. These things, I know, are important. And a year ago I walked into the sanctuary, and a young man sat quietly in a pew with tears running down his cheeks, just needing, I hope, to be quiet and in God's house in a time of grief. So I certainly do not mean to downplay the physical presence of God in brick and stone. When I am at church, though, I am a Sunday school teacher, a mother, a wife, and sometimes a coffee maker. I put on a dress and carefully spray my hair.

I like the me that frequents bars better than the Sunday school me; I hope God does too.

• • •

A Face in the Crowd: Points to Ponder

1. What are some of the problems with keeping things in your life "under wraps"?

2. Discuss ways that you can foster community within your neighborhood, church, or workplace.

3. What are some negatives associated with establishing community? For example, what happens if you attempt to establish a network of caring friends only to find that one member is always "fine" or "perfect"?

4. What do you do when you are lonely? Do you eat, call someone, read, exercise, watch TV, or just sit?

5. Who can you think of in the Bible, in leadership, or in your world who suffered with loneliness?

6. Read Psalms 6, 22, and 25. How can you feel closer to God?

Mutual Funds and Compounding Trust

"What the hell was it I wanted to buy, I wonder, that was worth—
Well, no matter. It's a late day for regrets."

—*Eugene O'Neill*, A Long Day's Journey into Night

IT USUALLY COMES THE FIRST WEEK IN DECEMBER. EVERY DAY that first week Wayne comes home and says, "Has it come yet?" When it arrives, I call him at work and let him know that it's the day. I wait until he comes home, and then I read it aloud. We try to keep a straight face upon the first reading, but we don't usually make it. The second reading we pause between sentences to guffaw.

It's the "Christmas Letter."

"Ashley" and "Brad" have perfect lives, perfect children, and two perfect vacation cruises a year. We are treated to "Caitlyn's" dance lesson days, "Colton's" extraordinary two-year-old command of the English language, and the goings-on of Ashley's branch of the Junior League. Brad is fast rising to the top of his company, and the SUV racks up the miles as Ashley lovingly drives the children to their private-school activities.

We shouldn't laugh, I know. But we really don't even know these people anymore. They were college sorority and fraternity friends, and we haven't seen them in over ten years. But somehow we manage to stay on their Christmas list; I cynically suspect so that Ashley can say to one of her friends, "I am so exhausted. I just sent out five thousand Christmas cards." So we're not really making fun of them (or so we tell ourselves), but rather we're making fun of what they represent.

We like to pretend to take the high road.

For me, reading the Christmas letter is always a reminder of the life I have chosen to leave behind. I relinquished keeping up with the Joneses a few years ago when I realized that I would rather travel to Europe than drive nice cars and have the latest in $300 purses. It was not always so. In college I pledged a sorority, dated a fraternity boy, and had the latest in upper-middle-class ware. I carried a $250 Gucci purse, a $100 Gucci billfold, and a $50 Gucci coin keeper. I don't remember what the key chain cost. I knew right down to a girl's shoes about how much her outfit cost and whether she was in style. My friends and I boasted that we could tell what sorority a girl was in by the clothes she wore. Then I went to class.

I never carried my Gucci purse to class. In class I listened to sociology professors talk about unfair distribution of wealth in the United States. I listened to English professors discuss the importance of the human heart, the human soul. I took notes as my psychology professors illustrated the need for humans to be accepted, to feel included. I kept my lives separate, but unequal. I was drawn to the intellectual side of life—toward the people who wore open-toed sandals and decade-old polyester suits because they truly did not care what they wore as long as it was comfortable. But I resisted the polyester path. I decided that I could be a caring human being and still care about fashion, about purses, about status.

And so I did for quite some time. My girls wore OshKosh outfits and Nike tennis shoes on their baby feet. But sometime in the years I was writing my dissertation I took a year off from the fashion/purse/shoe industry, and I still haven't caught back up. Sometime during the years of Kool-Aid stains and muddy shoes coming in from a glorious romp on the trampoline, I got sidetracked, forgot whether Dooney-Burke was in or out. Perhaps it was watching my dear friend die of cancer, slowly, painfully, without grace or mercy. Maybe it was the three days my daughter was in the hospital for asthma when I promised God that if she would just be all right, I would never ask for anything again. (Sorry up there, but I hope you understand.) I fell off the merry-go-round of perfection and success. Now from the park bench, just watching it go around makes me dizzy. So much time and effort go into that carnival ride that I no longer am willing to invest in it.

So when Ashley gushes about their latest Disney cruise, I envision the hours it must take to pack the right combination of outfits and hair bows. When she highlights her husband's success, I think of the nights I guess she spends alone while he works late or travels. I don't want her life anymore. And I'm sure she doesn't want mine.

I sometimes wear polyester, but, even more telling, I usually buy Payless shoes. I don't care what kind of car I drive; I just want it to run. I think that if Ashley could see me now, she might recoil in horror. I clip my nails to the quick, my hair needs a cutting, and my bedroom has the original wallpaper (gasp!) that was put on it twenty years ago. I just don't care about wallpaper much anymore. But I am saving up to take my kids to Europe. I went to New York City to see plays last month, and I donated a hundred dollars to the local women's shelter. My priorities have shifted. Usually when we say our priorities have shifted, we mean that we spend money differently. People often put their money into what they feel is most important: image, church, children.

In the last few years, my husband and I have sputtered to our feet financially. I suppose we could try to keep up with Ashley and Brad from a financial perspective, but we cannot from a values perspective. By this I do not mean to suggest that what they write about, what matters to them, is bad or unimportant. In many ways, they are achieving the American dream and working hard to do so. Many of us were handed a phantom script in college, and Ashley and Brad have followed the stage directions. And, to be honest, there are worse outlines to follow. Ashley is, I have no doubt, a caring mother. Brad is, I am sure, a hard worker and a devoted father/husband when he has time. I know Ashley depends on him to support her in the style to which he said, "I do." I just found, for me, that the script was too restrictive.

In a way I am greedier than Ashley and Brad. I want so many things beyond purses and shoes and cruises. I want to watch my children volunteer in a soup kitchen. I want them to know the New York City subway system. I want them to understand that some children their age have cystic fibrosis and it is a gift beyond measure to be healthy. I want them to have depth. For them to see the world is to understand that there is more than one way to live, love, find meaning. I want them to write their own script. For them to do that, I have to write mine. And I have found in attempting to write my own lines that I have very little interest anymore in wearing the latest designer shoes.

What we want in life, what we desire, often speaks of what we perceive that we lack. Thankfully, perhaps selfishly, my family has its needs covered. Sure there are first-edition books that I would like to buy, new Ping golf clubs for my husband. But what I want most desperately is meaning, to live an intentional life. I live in one of the most affluent counties in the United States, but I have to search for those with whom I can share an in-depth conversation. I am attempting to fashion a lifestyle that is filled with friends who share a similar vision, cultivate shared values. I don't want a life filled with stuff anymore; I want a life filled with moments.

I don't write a Christmas letter, but if I did, I wouldn't say much about vacations or promotions. Instead I would write about walking down the street on a beautiful May morning toward the St. Louis Art Museum to view the Van Gogh exhibit and feeling like life was just beginning. I'd write that I didn't know that at thirty-four I could still feel so much anticipation, so much hope, so much joy, on simply walking down a tree-lined street toward a museum. My Christmas letter would have to recount Erin's coming home from school and telling me that one of the little girls in her class had said something mean to a little girl "of lesser means" and that Erin herself told the mean little girl to leave the other one alone. Watching my child's eyes change as she told that story meant more to me than sixty sets of bone china. My Christmas letter would have to tell about my husband's coming home from work and saying, "We haven't really talked for a while. Let's go get a beer. The kids can have cereal for dinner." I suppose that my Christmas letter might appear a tad boring. And if I'm honest, and I try to be, there are many moments in the year of my life I want to forget: the night that I told Marybeth that she had a bad attitude and to "get her butt to bed right now," the time a student called at the wrong moment and I responded impatiently and dismissively.

But I don't write a Christmas letter, and I look forward every year to reading about my college acquaintance's perfect life. I know her life isn't always smooth, any more than mine is, but I cherish my newly found ability to let the tags show. They are usually clearance tags, or they come from Payless or maybe even Kohls. Meanwhile, my Europe travel account is growing, and if I'm lucky, my trust in my children's fundamental understanding of growing up to be people of compassion, of character, of interest, will compound.

• • •

Whine Stewards

Now the whole group of those who believed were of one heart and soul, and no one claimed private ownership of any possessions, but everything they owned was held in common. With great power the apostles gave their testimony to the resurrection of the Lord Jesus, and great grace was upon them all. There was not a needy person among them, for as many as owned lands or houses sold them and brought the proceeds of what was sold. They laid it at the apostles' feet, and it was distributed to each as any had need.

—*Acts 4:32-35*

WHY IS IT THAT I HAVE TO PAY $20.25 PER YEAR FOR RECYCLING? This is not fair. We go through six plastic gallon jugs of milk per week, seven days' worth of the Kansas City Star, numerous green bean cans, pop cans, occasional beer and wine bottles, a few magazines and *Wall Street Journals,* mountains of junk mail, and at least four yogurt containers every week. Toss in the odd salad dressing bottle or telephone book, and our little green bin is usually overflowing. We are doing our part to save the environment by living by the mantra "reduce, reuse, recycle." And now we have to pay for our good deeds? Where is the logic in this? Shouldn't we be encouraging people to recycle by making it free, rather than by making it a hindrance for them to care for the environment by making them pay for it?

There are two frightening problems with this logic. The first is that it costs money to recycle the plastic, run the trucks up and down the street, and pay the staff that dumps the little green bins into the big green truck. The money has to come from somewhere. It makes sense that it would come from *chez* consumer. We could request "the government" pay for it, but that also translates into you and me footing the bill.

The second problem with this logic is that, unfortunately, it makes some sense. Why recycle if I have to pay for it? Why not dump all those triangle-stamped containers in with the banana peels, coffee grounds, and used Kleenex and turn out the light in the garage and go to bed? It is easier, cheaper, and gives you more space for bikes and golf clubs.

So it is with the conundrum of how to live in the world. It is a choice of priority. If you are poor, you don't waste money paying the recycler. If you can afford it, you do it and feel virtuous. Or you drive to the nearest recycling station with your weekly load of recyclables and dump them in the appropriate holes (yeah, right).

Recycling is just one example of how we are conflicted about the "stuff" we have. I chuckled to myself when I overheard one wealthy philanthropist discussing with her husband the plan for getting a new computer for the bedroom. "I'll be able to log on to Greenpeace and download my flyers much faster," she said to her lunch companion as her husband put her on hold. "I can do the live chats and tell people about our fund-raising efforts. My computer is so old; we'll just have to throw it out. It works fine; it is just sooo slow."

Hmmm. What's wrong with this picture? It is an issue of not seeing the trees for the clear-cut forest in her case. She would be fine using her old computer. But she wanted a new one because it is faster. And the old one will be discarded.

We have enormous waste in our country. And we like it that way. I like it that way. I like it when my sandwich is wrapped in a sandwich bag. I like it when my Diet Coke cap twists off the little plastic ring so I know it hasn't been tampered with. I was thrilled with disposable diapers and used them several times a day for over eight years. I drive over twelve thousand miles per year in my car and rarely take it out of town. I throw away the shrink-wrap from raw chicken by surrounding it with the Styrofoam meat tray it comes in, bundling it with the absorbent pad they stick under the chicken, wrapping it in the paper towel I used to wipe up the juice, and putting that inside a grocery sack, which goes into a plastic bag in my kitchen trash, which is carried out into the blue trash can in my garage. This is nuts!

We buy AA batteries by the four dozen and throw them away when they are used up. We buy and then break or lose interest in plastic toys when we get fast food kid's meals (food which is wrapped and sacked for your dining pleasure).

We are wasteful. We have been conditioned to be wasteful. We enjoy what we see as the benefits of being a disposable society.

My kids have had whining spells of wanting another Nintendo game, more marbles, a bigger TV, a bigger collection of Beanie Babies. I have the usual conversations with them about money, the cost of those things, how they can earn their own money to get some of the things they want, and how it all works. And then some days I get so fed up I think the only solution is to move to a place where kids pick up scraps for food, drink, bathe, and wash their clothing in the same water.

We never see the effects of our poor stewardship of resources. We just like that things are clean. (Why is gum wrapped three times in those Plen-T-Paks?)

Nobody likes to hear sermons on money. I don't particularly like preaching them either. But I do feel the message boiling in my veins about stewardship—another churchy word, I know, but the right one. Stewardship means understanding what you have been given and being responsible about how you use and maintain it: whether it is cash, turning off the lights, or dragging Main Street all night with your friends in a gas-guzzling SUV.

We have a consumer mentality that makes us want to be first in line, get all the "stuff" for ourselves, and throw away what we don't need. We don't see polluted water (much), polluted air (well, maybe a little), or trash-strewn highways (we don't?). We typically are able to avoid the fallout of our own wastefulness. Or at least we think so.

We can claim that "it takes a village" to raise a child but forget that the earth is all we have. I have finally trained myself to turn off the faucet while brushing my teeth. I knew it was important, but I changed mostly because my son learned that trick in his elementary school class and he kept bugging me until I changed my bad habit.

Maybe that's the ecologist's role or the preacher's or the educator's—to pester us until we change our habits. I do see all that we have as a gift. I guess what I really am, then, is an ingrate. I don't appreciate it. Of course, I certainly would whine and wail if all these necessities were suddenly gone, but I don't truly expect that unless there is a nuclear winter. I wonder how flawed that logic is.

Every Monday morning, my toddlers would hear the rumble in the street and ask me, "Is it big truck day?" I would answer yes, and we would race to the front door to see the garbage men driving first the recycling truck and then the trash truck through the neighborhood, picking up the week's load. The kids' sticky hands would make perfect prints on my glass front door as they watched in awe the men and one woman hustle around with the goods. They would press their noses up to the glass as the trucks passed by, trying to see them as far as they could as they lumbered down the road.

When the excitement died down, I would get out the plastic bottle of Windex, spray the door, wipe it with a paper towel, and throw the waste in the trash for them to pick up the next week.

Paying Dues: Points to Ponder

1. Was there any material object you really wanted as a child that you did not receive? What was it? How did this experience affect you?

2. How much does money influence how you set your priorities?

3. What would you drive if you could drive any kind of vehicle?

4. Do you give regularly to your church or other charitable (not-for-profit) organizations?

5. Which Scripture passages could help you to "stand firm" for what you believe?

6. Psalm 24:1 reads, "The earth is the LORD's and all that is in it, the world, and those who live in it." How would you apply this verse to your life?

Retreat

"Many women have done excellently, but you surpass them all."
Charm is deceitful, and beauty is vain,
but a woman who fears the LORD is to be praised.
Give her a share in the fruit of her hands,
and let her works praise her in the city gates.
—*Proverbs 31:29-31*

I RECENTLY ATTENDED A CLERGYWOMEN'S RETREAT. YOU KNOW, one of those touchy-feely events designed to help us "bond" as sisters in the faith. Share your angst, be validated in who you are, learn coping skills, and glean some new material to plagiarize for your next children's sermon—that was the purpose as I saw it when I was asked to lead the Bible study portion of the weekend. The thing about clergywomen is that they are strange birds. Myself included. Have you ever met one that you really thought you could relate to on anything but a surfacey-churchy level?

I must admit that preachers in general present the public with a conundrum. On one hand, they are caring, loving people who are present in your hour of need, pray over your sick grandmother, hold hands with small children, and sing "Kum ba Yah." Very endearing. On the other hand, the clergy wear funny clothes. Either they are dressed to the nines in blue-blazer-khaki-pants salesman garb (complete with pinkie rings), or they don a bizarre ensemble of faded shirts with food stains and buttons missing and black socks with dress shoes. And those are the men. The women are worse. They run the gamut from pancake makeup, thick mascara, and lacy-collared dresses bedecked with golden jewelry to running around sagging braless in a faded T-shirt, long skirt, tennis shoes, and dark socks. (What is it with the dark socks? Did I miss that class in seminary?)

And preachers' ideas ... well they are so ... strange. Clergywomen seem to be either an extreme of militant feminist with a huge chip on her shoulder or a warm, fuzzy, "God loves you" type, which is of little or no help when your daughter got cut from the soccer team and you need advice on how to deal with it. They see the world differently than most people and are sometimes difficult to engage in conversation. They default to preaching if they are trying to convince or persuade you, or they listen attentively like a therapist with appropriate "I see," or "Hmmm ... that must have made you feel terrible." There never seems to be much middle ground.

At any rate, a gaggle of clergywomen camping together for a weekend is my idea of combat duty. But I accepted the invitation to lead as part of "the deal" in becoming a minister of word and sacrament. You do stuff you don't want to do, and you don't get paid for it. That's the deal.

Imagine my surprise when these thirty or so women came together in what I considered a delightful time of conversation and sharing. We shared some of our struggles of being female clergy. Some complained of being underpaid and overworked. (Take a number, girls). Others had concerns of sexual harassment in the workplace perpetrated by the very membership we are trying to reach for Christ. Everyone laughed at the thought of zipping along preaching a sermon when someone's infant cries in the front row, your milk lets down, and over the front of your Geneva robe spreads a warm flow of mother's milk you were storing for your own baby to let flow after the 11:00 service.

But the most poignant memory I had of that experience was the exercise we did in "what if?" What if the patriarchal society that we now recognize to be in place, and was in place at the various times Scripture was penned, were different? What if women made the rules? What if women were "in power" and laid out the strategy? What if women set up the first house churches? What if women instead of men designed pastoral care, preaching, worship, and the sacraments? What if?

There were some good responses. First, you can be sure no Moses would have wandered in the wilderness for forty years. A woman leader would have stopped and asked directions. So many a tribe and nation would not have ended violently. Peace would have been discussed around the hearth and a compromise achieved. There would have been more talking, less fighting. And the whole thing would have been tidier, not so cluttered—clean toilet bowls and all that, fewer beheadings. And once a month, we would all get a week off.

We batted around a few ideas. But my epiphany came when I realized that if women had set up the whole thing, it would still be flawed. It would be equally broken. Men don't have the corner on selfishness, pride, and bad ideas. Women would have made mistakes of colossal proportions as well; we would just take more time to talk about it afterward. We would have talked the things to death, related to and heard every voice, and had guilt over whether everyone felt included.

Can it be that the problems we blame men for exist simply because they got there first and came up with the first ideas? Because we have come along later, only to critique and criticize? Sometimes we don't give our men enough credit.

• • •

Washing Angry Dishes

It is not the anger of other women that will destroy us but our refusals to stand still, to listen to its rhythms, to learn within it, to move beyond the manner of presentation to the substance, to tap that anger as an important source of empowerment.

—*Audre Lorde,* Sister Outsider

I HAD MY PARENTS OVER FOR DINNER LAST NIGHT. WE HAD salmon with a cucumber-dill sauce, fresh sweet corn from the farmer's market, and pasta with pesto. We had a garden salad resplendent with homegrown basil, English cucumbers, and mushrooms. It was a lovely meal, but in my rushing around I left the salmon on the grill a bit too long, and some of us had blackened salmon. All in all, it tasted very good.

After dinner my mother and I washed dishes while my father and Wayne took the girls golfing on the local par-three course. We were washing dishes by hand, because there were so many of them and my dishwasher is mediocre at best, when it hit me. Right in the middle of sudsing a small saucepan I felt the famil-iar frustration that, if properly paid its due, becomes anger.

I have long felt that among women depression is anger

turned inside on the self. And, in our culture, women learn young that anger is dangerous. Societal words teach women at an early age to hide anger. "Bitch on wheels" is one that I remember; "bitter old woman," another. Women who display anger are often deemed "on the rag" or "needing to get laid." I once asked a friend whose husband had gone on a weekend "retreat" leaving her with two small children if she was angry about the fact that spouses were not allowed at the party. "Oh no, not at all," she told me brightly, "He works very, very hard. He deserves some time off." She then polished off about three glasses of wine telling me all the while about her wonderful life. She drowned her anger, but I think, more tellingly, she did not allow herself even to admit to it. Later her young son dropped a glass of Kool-Aid on the floor, and she flew at him in fury, sending him to his room and making him feel as if he had committed a terrible crime. "He has to learn not to be so clumsy," she told me, wiping up the mess.

Now, I am not pointing fingers here. Truly. I will even concede that her husband did work hard and was entitled to some time away. But so did she. The anger that women feel and have felt has historically been sublimated. When we are angry, we often apologize for our anger as if we were excessive or our feelings were inappropriate. It took me years to recognize and give voice to my anger in a healthy way. In the early years of our marriage, I would hold in all the instances that made me angry, and then Wayne would leave a glass on the kitchen counter, and it would all come pouring out in ways that were, in fact, inappropriate. A wonderful book by Harriet Lerner called The *Dance of Anger* helped me to understand that often I had the right to be angry, but I did not, in fact, have the right to hold it in and then use it as a weapon when it grew too excessive.

Over the years I have learned to deal with my anger like I deal with the dishes. If I let them pile up, then they seem overwhelming. However, if I do them regularly, they seem manageable, and I feel like my house is clean and well kept. I also listen carefully for that nudge of frustration that precipitates anger for me. I work full-time, do almost all of the housecleaning and child raising as well as regularly having those we care about over to dinner. All of these aspects of my life are important to me, but I share my life with someone who often takes the clean house, nutritious dinner, and usually emotionally well-balanced children for granted. It is the work that traditionally was called "women's work" and for which there was and still is no financial reward. My husband works many hours. I appreciate his hard work. But he also receives a large financial compensation for his work; for his time and energy he regularly is taken out to lunch, dinner, and sporting events.

I don't begrudge him these gratuities, but I also know that if I want to remain healthy, I must reward myself so that I don't become one of those "bitter" women. When I sense my anger and am tired of cleaning the house, I call a cleaning service. Yes, it is expensive, but so is feeling used and unappreciated. I cook foods that I like, not just ones that the kids will eat. In short, although our society historically expects women to do a great deal of work for which they are not expected to demand or receive compensation, I do speak out, both in words and with actions. Contrary to making me bitter or hateful, acknowledging and giving voice to my anger create a more peaceful and caring household. I saw a woman wearing a T-shirt the other day that said, "If Mama Ain't Happy, Ain't Nobody Happy." We live in a society where women are much more likely to be depressed than men. We need to learn to make women happier, but in order to do that women have to acknowledge the pressure points in their lives—and the corresponding anger. Then they can develop individual plans to mitigate the pressure and address the anger.

I cooked a wonderful dinner last night for six people. I created a safe and stable environment for my children; they delighted in my parents' praise and interest in their lives. I made the world a bit better place in which to live and love. So this morning I packed the girls off to the golf course with pocket money to buy lunch at the course. And I made a big pot of coffee and read the paper in lovely quiet. I did not answer the phone. I did not pay bills. I cared for myself.

And tomorrow I'm going to shop for a better dishwasher.

• • •

Me, Tarzan: Points to Ponder

1. What are three things you blame men for? Have you harbored resentment over them?
2. What can you do to break the habit of "male bashing"?
3. What does your spouse do that causes you anger?
4. When has being angry produced a positive result? How so?
5. Who cooks meals in your household? Does this cause conflict?
6. First Corinthians 14:33-36 says women should keep silent in church, while Galatians 3:28 says in Christ there is no male or female. How do you reconcile these verses? How has your church tradition dealt with this issue?

Living With the Sinners

for life's not a paragraph
and death i think is no parenthesis

—*e. e. cummings*, "since feeling is first"

A GOOD FRIEND DIED THE OTHER DAY FROM BREAST CANCER. Teri left behind a nine-month-old baby and a husband. And I am so angry at her. She wouldn't accept the possibility of death, even when she knew she was dying. She kept telling us all that she was going to be fine, even though we knew she wasn't. Because she never let anyone behind her iron curtain, I never really knew if she was okay, or as okay as a person could be about dying at forty-one and leaving behind a baby. She died, and I never got to ask her if she wanted me to send birthday presents every year to her son for her. I wanted to bring her cards for each year of his life and have her sign them and write a note for Hunter at two, three, ten, sixteen, twenty-one. She thought up until the end that God was going to save her. Or at least she pretended that she believed that God was going to save her, which amounted to the same thing. And when she died, I was, am, mad at God for not answering her prayers. I never expected God to answer mine.

At the visitation Teri was outfitted in a hideous purple dress that she would have hated and the wig that she threw off the moment she entered the house (one day she put the wig on the bald baby and took pictures). Driving home from the visitation, Wayne said to me, "She must have thought over and over, why me?" This perspective threw me off guard—not only because I never heard Teri utter those words, or even thoughts, but instead because it was a question that I have never asked. My fears, upon waiting on a blood test or biopsy, have run along the lines of "Why not me?" Some of the very best people I know have been felled by cancer, mental illness, car wrecks. In fact, I used to comfort myself with the song "Only the Good Die Young" when I sat in fear in waiting rooms or holding an unopened envelope that contained test results.

Recently my daughter read the biography of the teenage girl who, when the gun wielder at Columbine asked her if she believed in God, said yes and was promptly shot in the head. I said to my daughter, "If you are ever in that situation, you tell whoever holds that gun that you worship the same god or gods that he does. You do not self-sacrifice." She was startled, I think, by my anger, my vehemence. "Geez, Mom," she said, "you want me to say that I don't believe in God?" I nodded vigorously, "In that situation, yes. Don't die to prove that God exists. Either God does or doesn't, and your death isn't going to make any difference in proving that. But your death would be such a tragic loss to me and the rest of the world." She rolled her eyes, but I could tell she was uneasy. She wants to be a good girl and do the right thing. I, on the other hand, have watched a whole slew of women die physically and/or emotionally by attempting to be good girls.

My friend told me that she could not go to the M. D. Anderson Cancer Center because she and her husband did not have the money. When her husband had cancer, he went to the Mayo

Clinic. When she had cancer, there was no money for second opinions, only money for new tractors and acreage. I begged her to let me take her to M. D. Anderson. I told her I would pay for it. She laughed, told me that God had led her to her doctor and that she was going to be fine. I went home, drank a bottle of wine, and cursed women who take care of everyone but themselves. My favorite lines from Billy Joel's "Only the Good Die Young" go, "I'd rather laugh with the sinners than cry with the saints / The sinners have much more fun / Darlin' only the good die young." Only, in my case, it's not only the fact that the sinners have more fun; they also survive—or at least if they die, they generally do it on their own terms.

At the funeral at the fundamentalist Baptist church that Teri and her husband of two years attended, all the speakers said that Teri died a "woman of God." And we're supposed to find peace in that? When men die, do women stand up and say placidly, "We'll miss him, but he was a man of God"? Who cares? A smart, witty, funny, insightful woman who dedicated her life to educating young people died, and these men stand at the podium and command that if there is a person in the audience who has not allowed Jesus into his or her heart, now would be a good time. All I can think is that Teri will never be able to sing the "Itsy Bitsy Spider" to her baby and watch him attempt to make his fingers climb the waterspout. And I think that if she would have told her husband to go to hell and her oncologist to go to hell and listened to me, because I know that no one really cares when women die, then maybe she would have gone to M. D. Anderson and maybe she wouldn't have died—or at least wouldn't have died so gruesomely. Her body at the end looked like the bodies of the Holocaust victims that I have seen in documentaries and in my nightmares. Both breasts were gone, and her chest was covered with massive lumps of scar tissue. Her back and chest were covered with third-degree burns from all the radiation. Her hands and legs were puffy from cortisone shots. Her lungs were filled with cancer and with fluid. She did not die easily, nor did prayers seem to make any difference.

I know that men die horrible, pain-filled deaths. I know that men become depressed and feel they have no purpose. I know they're out there because the statistics keep telling me so. I just haven't met any of them. The men I know take care of themselves pretty damn well. I think that taking care of oneself is a good thing. I just wish the women I know did more of it. I wish that I did more of it, and I take care of myself better than most. But, then, I have never professed to being good.

I learned young what happens to women who are too good. They die—usually young.

. . .

Buried Feelings

"He will wipe every tear from their eyes.
Death will be no more;
mourning and crying and pain will be no more,
for the first things have passed away."

—*Revelation 21:4*

ONE OF THE THINGS ON MY TO-DO LIST TODAY IS TO PREPARE A funeral service. Actually, I should refer to it as, not a funeral, but a "service in witness to the resurrection of Jesus Christ in memory of Francis Shlichter." I've never met Francis. He was a member of my church for many years but moved to Salt Lake City before I became pastor here. I don't know anything about him other than what I read in the obituary and the fact that he was a Christian and a member of my church.

Some of the members will remember him, and I'll ask them things about him so I can prepare a more personal eulogy. But this will be one of the easier memorial services I perform since I didn't know him. There have been some I thought I wouldn't be able to speak through.

My first memorial service was one of my most difficult. It was for Dora Schultz, a girl from Glassboro, New Jersey, who had just turned twenty-one. She had a genetic disorder that robbed her first of her motor skills, then her speech, and finally her life. Her mother, father, sister, and brother had been her twenty-four-hour caretakers for twenty-one years, the last five of which were particularly difficult. It was hard to grasp the reality of this tragic death and compose myself enough to say something meaningful and halfway inspiring. I still keep in contact with this family after ten years, mostly because of the impression that memorial service made on me.

I remember the service for the young woman whose name I don't recall and whose disease I never understood. All I remember is the fact that she had both legs amputated in an attempt to save her life. It didn't.

I remember the tears that flowed as I watched one family prepare to bury their matriarch. The children placed flowers, toys, teddy bears, and a "World's Best Grandma" sweatshirt in the casket as we all sobbed at the loss of a wonderful woman. I can't remember her name either, but I empathized with the family as I watched those children.

I remember very well the memorial service for Dody Millikan. She was buried on August 20, 1997. The day of her service, I was two weeks away from my due date to deliver my third child. I had been to a doctor's appointment that day at 9 A.M., did the funeral at 11 A.M., and began having contractions during the committal service. The funeral director hustled me out of the mausoleum and into the waiting sedan and watched me drive away as he wrung his hands. Diana Victoria Dolquist was born at 6:13 that evening. A busy day.

I remember George Granberry's service. I had to sit in a pew before the service and cry long and loud at his death from esophageal cancer. The funeral director got a bit nervous when it was only fifteen minutes before the service was to begin and the minister was wailing in the front pew. I was able to compose myself in time, and whatever chemical is released in your brain after a good cry helped me to make it through the service with a stiff upper lip. I didn't lose it again until I did the final benediction. I offered three tributes to him from the three things that shaped his life. He was an active Boy Scout leader, so I gave him the Boy Scout salute. He served his country in the army in Korea and in the navy in World War II, so I gave him a military salute. He was a Christian leader, so I closed his service with the sign of the cross. Then I cried some more.

I marveled at George's widow, Pat. She was certainly rocked by her husband's death, but she had an assurance and a "peace that surpasses all understanding" as she and George took the journey together through his illness and death. They had a faith that God was in control and it was all in God's perfect timing. I have to say that if I were in her shoes, I suspect I might have been spending more time cursing than praising. But she ministered to me in her strength. When she got her own diagnosis of breast cancer three years later, I watched her at work again. With quiet strength and dignity, she persevered, had surgery and radiation, and is fit and fine, now a year later.

I almost always cry at funerals—either before or after, sometimes during. I always wear waterproof mascara on funeral days. When my grandparents died, I did not officiate; I mourned. But whenever someone who has touched your life dies, the loss is real, even if you don't remember his or her name.

I cannot imagine how much worse the losses might be if I did not have faith of my own. Because I have attended and officiated at so many funerals, memorial services, "services in witness to the resurrection of Jesus Christ in memory of Jane Doe," and visitations, I have a deep sense that death is part of life. I understand the rhythms of life in a different way. I wouldn't be caught dead as a funeral director because that job is all about loss and sadness and watching people part with loved ones, not to mention watching them part with a big wad of cash. At least in my job I get to see babies born, perform weddings, and reconcile differences.

I seldom get angry at death anymore. This might be partly because I have started skipping this stage and head straight for sadness—I being one who likes to do things efficiently. Or it might be because I am more philosophical about death. And I don't see death as the enemy. Wearing my pastor's robe I have said many times, "There are worse things than dying." I believe that. Suffering endlessly or needlessly is worse. Rotting in a hospital or nursing home is worse. Being imprisoned in a useless body but with a sharp mind is worse. Death can be a relief.

But the main reason I no longer fear death is because I truly believe that death does not have the final word. I do believe that there is more. I do believe that Jesus' death on the cross was the last death we mourn because it was followed by his resurrection, which gives us hope. We have been promised eternal life, and I plan to get it. Pat and George knew that. That is what made them have comfort through their tears.

I can't imagine being defeated by death. It is not the victor; Jesus is. It is a transition, not the "final answer."

I miss the people who have touched my life. And I am grateful they have come my way. And I will continue to send other souls on their way as they pass through death to life eternal. Sniffling as I preach, I have great hope.

• • •

Dying to Live: Points to Ponder

1. Have you made a last will and testament? If not, what is preventing you from doing so?
2. What is your greatest fear about death and dying?
3. What deaths have affected you the most? Why?
4. Has the death of someone close to you ever caused you to question your faith?
5. In what ways do you "blame God" for the losses in your life? What are you really feeling about those losses?
6. What does Scripture say about death and afterlife? Read 1 Corinthians 15. What does that say to you about hope?